Generations
Of
Good Food

Generations Of Good Food

Eleanor Gaccetta

ReadersMagnet, LLC

This book is a collection of recipes spanning several generations of my mother's family, our friends, and relatives. These home cooks could easily have rivaled a professional chef or baker.

I published my book, *One Caregiver's Journey*, in March of 2018. It is a memoir about the 9 ½ years I spent providing 24/7 care for my mother. She died in May of 2017. This book was conceived during the winter of 2017 when a couple of weeks of cold temperatures and harsh weather conditions in Colorado required me to hunker down and stay indoors. I compiled my late mother's cookbooks and favorite recipes and assembled them into a cookbook for her granddaughters, young family members, and close friends. The book is the fruit of my labor. I hope you enjoy preparing and eating the many family recipes contained in *Generations of Good Food*. Visit www.onecaregiversjourney.com for more information about my caregiving book.

Like *One Caregiver's Journey*, this book is dedicated to my family and especially to my brother, Don. The support and love I have received for my caregiving efforts and for the writing and publishing of my book, are immeasurable. The world would be void without them.

It is with humble gratitude that I also dedicate this book to my Filipino family. Without their support to market and promote *One Caregiver's Journey* and their friendships after meeting in Miami, the endeavor to publish this personal cookbook might not have occurred. Even though they are half a world away, I will always cherish their friendship.

FORWARD

At one time cooking and baking were skills necessary for survival. Today cooking a meal or baking a dessert from scratch is considered an art. My mother, Marianne, was the eldest daughter of six children. She did not work the family farm like her three sisters. She stayed behind with her grandmother to help clean the house and by extension to learn how to cook and bake. They cooked three meals a day for the family and all the workers who supported their farm. They did not break out breakfast bars, make smoothies, or toss a box of cereal and milk on the table. There was no fast food or Uber-eats for delivery. The kitchens had no modern appliances like a microwave or food processor, and they faced stacks of dishes to wash by hand after each meal. My great-grandmother taught my grandmother and my mother to cook and bake; they in turn taught all their daughters and granddaughters. Thus, the title of this book, **Generations of Good Food.** My mother was a masterful cook and baker. How fortunate we were to have had such an amazing influence in our lives.

When my mother married my father in 1937, they lived with his family consisting of his parents, two married brothers, their children, and two single brothers. One of my aunts always said it was a great day for the Irish when my mother joined that family–even though they were all Italian. My grandfather learned quickly that my mother knew how to cook and bake. He gave her free reign to use as much butter and eggs as necessary to ensure the family had sweet treats for their daily afternoon coffee break. Mom often recounted how each week she would bake a 5 gallon can of spritz cookies along with assorted cakes and pies. How many cookies would it take to fill a 5 gallon can? She and my grandmother also baked 16 loaves of bread each week in an outdoor oven for family meals. They often said that there wasn't a single vegetable in the garden that couldn't be sautéed with garlic and olive oil or served with pasta. Today households don't have 15 to 20 people; but they do eat.

Can you cook and bake? Or do you rely on store-bought prepared foods? Only a handful of my generation still enjoys the art of cooking and baking like my mother and grandmother did. Today households are busy and hectic. Meal planning is whatever is easiest and quickest. My hope is that you will take the time to find a recipe that stimulates your taste buds and motivates you to step back in time and cook or bake like in the old days.

Some recipes are easy, others are not. But one thing is for sure: they have all been made with love to be enjoyed by those who are loved. Food is love, so dive in and enjoy.

Eleanor Gaccetta

CONTENTS

MAIN DISHES AND MISCELLANEOUS

Alfredo Sauce for Pasta. 3
Auntie Ann's Pretzel. 4
Avocado, Grapefruit and Romain Salad 5
Avocado Toast. 6
Baked Shrimp. 7
Barbeque Ribs. 8
Basic Pizza Dough 9
Basil Roasted Chicken with Garlic Sauce 10
Boccalino's Caesar Salad. 11
Braciole 12
Homemade Quick Breakfast. 13
Canning Dill Pickles 14
Canning Sweet Pickles 15
Caponata 16
Cheese Pineapple Salad 18
Crab Bisque Soup 19
Crab Cakes. 20
Easy Sunday Pot Roast 21
Mrs. Olquin's Enchiladas 22
Crusty Fish Sticks from Fresh Fish. 23
Grandma Spano's Eggplant 25
True Southern Fried Chicken 27
Garlic Jam 28
Quick American Green Chile. 29
Homemade Chicken Soup 30
Italian Breading for Beef, or Lamb 31
Italian Chicken Fingers 32
Italian Pork Rolls 33

Linguine with Clam Sauce 34
Mandarin Salad 36
Omaha White Chile. 37
Panzanella Salad. 38
Homemade Pasta 40
Pasta with Cheese and Pepper. 41
Pasta Fisherman Style. 42
Pasta with Lentils 43
Pasta with Olive Oil and Garlic 44
Pasta Salad 45
Pasta with Peas and Hamburger 46
Basil Pesto 48
Polenta 49
Italian Potato Salad. 50
American Potato Salad 51
Party Punch 52
Quiche Lorraine 53
Red Chile 54
Homemade Ricotta Cheese. 55
Ricotta Gnocchi 56
Creamy Ricotta Pasta with Spinach 57
Roasted Red Pepper Dip. 58
St. Lucy Day Rice Balls 59
Spicy Glazed Pecans. 61
Italian Spinach – Side Dish. 62
Spinach Sausage Quiche. 63
Steamed Dumplings 64
Stuffed Artichokes 65
Sautéed Mushrooms and Stuffed Mushrooms. 67
Tomato, Artichoke and Basil Pasta 68
Turkey Tetrazzini 69
Tuscan White Bean Chicken Soup 70

Whole Baked Chicken 71
Vegetarian Sandwich for One 72
Yummy Roasted Potatoes 73

BREADS AND DESSERT

Aunt Mella's Banana Bread. 76
Banana Muffins 77
Refrigerated Banana Split Dessert 78
Bran Muffins 79
Homemade Breadsticks 80
Cinnamon Rolls 81
Cream Puffs 82
Basic Crepes 83
Glorified Rice Salad 84
Grebbles 85
Ice Box Dessert. 86
Italian Ricotta Cheese Pie. 87
Peachy Marmalade 89
Poticia 90
Peanut Butter Pie 92
Sweet Easter Bread 93
Sweet Muffins 95
Sweet Cheese Muffins 96
Fruit Pie 97
Meringue for Pies 99
Sandy's Pie Crust 100
Super Pie Crust. 101

CAKES

Make Your Own Vanilla Extract 106
Homemade Frosting. 107
Apple Loaf Cake. 108

Apple Upside Down Cake 109
Better than Sex Cake 110
Carrot Cake 111
Semi-Homemade Carrot Cake 112
Cheesecake 113
Chocolate Almond Cheesecake. 114
Chiffon Cake 115
Chocolate Cake from Scratch 117
Chocolate Cherry Cake. 119
Cinnamon Chocolate Chip Cake 120
Dirt Cake 121
Old Fashioned Donuts 122
Dump Cake 123
Perfect Fudge Brownies 124
Fudge Frosting 125
German Chocolate Cake. 126
Coconut Frosting 128
Milky Way Cake. 129
Homemade Pineapple Upside Down Cake 130
Pumpkin Cheesecake 131
Bunny Cakes for Easter. 132
Marshmallow Frosting 133
Rhubarb Cake. 134
Bicardi Rum Cake 135
Royal Coconut Cake. 136
Walnut Glory Cake. 138
Zeppole (Italian Donuts) 139

COOKIES

Almond Lace Cookies 144
Basic Shortbread. 145
Baklava Puffs 146

Berry Shortbread Dreams 147
Biscotti (Almond Bars) 148
Cake Cookies 149
Chocolate Chip Cookies 150
Home Run Chocolate Chip Cookies 151
Chocolate Ricotta Cookies 152
Cinnamon-Sugar Spirals 153
Coconut Macaroons 154
Coconut Macaroons 155
Cracked Chocolate Cookies 156
Cream Cheese Chocolate Chip Cookies 157
Cowboy Cookies 158
"Cucidata" Italian Filled Cookies 159
Hello Dollies 160
Honey Cookies 161
Honey Sand Balls 163
John's Soft Chocolate Chip Cookies 164
Italian Knots 165
Lemon Cookies 166
Lemon Ricotta Cookies 167
Malted Milk Shortbread Cookies 168
Mocha Logs 169
(Naked) Ricotta Cookies 170
Aunt Jennie's Oatmeal Cookies 171
Regular Oatmeal Cookies 173
Pecan Cutout Cookies 174
Pecan Fingers 175
Pecan Sandie Cookies 176
Pizzelles 177
Pumpkin Cookies 178
Shortbread Cookie Bars with Salted Caramel 179
Pioneer Woman Sugar Cookies 180

Rosettes 181
Rum Balls 182
Scrupeds 183
Sesame Seed Cookies 184
Snickerdoodles 186
Spritz Cookies 187
Sweet Butter Cookies 188
Sweet Butter Cookie Alternatives 190
Sour Cream Twists 191
Ultimate Chocolate Chip Cookies 192
Walnut Horn Cookies 193
Whipped Spritz Cookies 194
Wine Cookies 195

CANDY

Angel Kisses 199
Cherry Cream Cheese Candy 200
Chocolate Peanut Clusters 201
Cream Cheese Candies 202
Coconut Joys 203
Date Balls 204
Easy Fudge 205
Liz's Fudge 206
Mrs. See's Fudge 207
Peanut Butter Snowballs 208
Potato Chip Clusters 209
Three Chocolate Fudge 210
Tiger Butter 211

Main Dishes and Miscellaneous

This section is dedicated to pasta dishes, salads, and other recipes. I hope you can make and enjoy some of them.

GENERATION 1

Great Grandmother Anna Petrucci-Spano – mom second from left Photo 1920

GENERATION 2

Sam and Antoinette Spano Family Mom's family –mom is the eldest daughter (Photo 1924)

ALFREDO SAUCE FOR PASTA

Cook the pasta of your choice in salted boiling water according to instructions. While the pan is heating to a boil make the sauce:

Sauce:

In a saucepan on low heat combine:

1 cup ricotta cheese

1 cube softened butter

1 ½ Tablespoons Romano cheese

2 Tablespoons fresh parsley chopped

Salt and Pepper to taste

Stir constantly to incorporate all ingredients into a smooth sauce. Turn the stove off, leave the pan on the burner to remain warm. Pour small amount of pasta water in your serving dish and drain pasta. Add pasta to the serving dish and pour sauce over and toss to incorporate the liquid.

AUNTIE ANN'S PRETZEL

Preheat oven to 450⁰

Step 1:

1 ½ cups warm water

1 ½ packages rapid rise yeast

2 Tablespoons brown sugar

1 1/8 teaspoon salt

4 cups all-purpose flour.

Sprinkle yeast in lukewarm water in a mixing bowl. Stir to dissolve. Add sugar and salt. Using dough hook on mixer, add flour and mix to a smooth, elastic dough. Put in a warm please to rise 1 ½ hours.

Step 2:

2 cups warm water

2 Tablespoons baking soda

While dough is rising mix water and baking soda in a bowl, stirring often.

After dough rises, pinch off pieces and roll them into long ropes and shape into pretzels. Dip in baking soda bath and place on a greased baking sheet. Allow to rise a second time.

Bake for 10 minutes until golden brown. Brush with 2-4 Tablespoons melted butter and sprinkle with coarse salt or coat with cinnamon sugar.

Eleanor Gaccetta

AVOCADO, GRAPEFRUIT AND ROMAIN SALAD

One head of Romain lettuce washed and chopped
2 Grapefruit peeled and sectioned

3 Avocados sectioned and cut

Citrus Dressing:

1 large shallot diced

2 Tablespoons of *seasoned* rice vinegar

1 Tablespoon lemon juice

1 Tablespoon orange juice

¼ cup olive oil

¼ teaspoon each lemon and orange zest

Place lettuce, grapefruit, and avocado in a bowl. Mix dressing and pour over greens. Toss to coat.

AVOCADO TOAST

2 Slices of bread toasted – your favorite bread will do!

1 clove garlic peeled and cut in half

¼ teaspoon olive oil

1 Avocado smashed

Salt and Pepper to taste

Toast bread. Rub fresh garlic over toast and brush with olive oil. Spread ½ mashed avocado over oil. Add salt, and pepper. This is good for breakfast or lunch or toast can be quartered for an appetizer.

Eleanor Gaccetta

BAKED SHRIMP

The traditional Italian Christmas Eve feast includes shrimp. Growing up, frying shrimp was a mess with oil, flour, and seasonings. The stove had to be cleaned before continuing with the meal preparation. My sister-in-law, Jackie, found this recipe one year and it became the shrimp staple for every Christmas Eve dinner thereafter. Baked shrimp is a great choice for a meal with friends anytime during the year. It is a one-pot meal with no mess to clean and it can be served with pasta.

Heat oven to 375^0

4 pounds of large (21-25) shrimp, deveined, shells and tail removed

1 cube butter melted

1 package Good Seasons Italian dressing mix (dry not bottle)

2 cups seasoned breadcrumbs–browned.

2 Tablespoons Olive oil

Brown the breadcrumbs in a non-stick skillet on medium with 2 Tablespoons olive oil. Stirring frequently until the crumbs are evenly, lightly browned. This process takes about 8 minutes. Set aside.
Put the melted butter in a roast pan, add shrimp and toss to coat with butter. Sprinkle dressing mix and breadcrumbs on top and mix again turning with a large spoon to coat all the shrimp.
Cover and bake for 30-35 minutes turning (stirring once) to make sure the shrimp in the middle can cook. Shrimp will be pink.

BARBEQUE RIBS

Preheat oven to 250^0

2 racks of baby back ribs

3 Tablespoons Kosher salt

1 Tablespoon black pepper

3 cloves garlic sliced

OR desired prepared rub

To prepare ribs, remove silver skin from back or under side of ribs. Pat dry with paper towels and cover with salt, and pepper and place slices of garlic throughout, or rub with prepared rub mixture liberally.

Tightly wrap ribs in sheets of plastic wrap and then two layers of aluminum foil. Place on a cookie sheet and bake for 2 1/2 hours.

Remove from foil and plastic wrap. Can put on grill and baste with BBQ sauce until a slight crust forms. Another option is to place ribs back on foil and baste with BBQ sauce under the oven broiler.

BASIC PIZZA DOUGH

When I was working and my mother was home, she would often have after school visits from my nieces and their children. Mom would know in advance and always prepared a treat for them. This basic pizza dough was something she could prepare quickly. Sometimes she would bake a pizza but most often she would double the recipe, fry it, and serve with sugar or honey. The grand and great-grandchildren have wonderful memories of these visits.

2 ½ cups all-purpose flour

1 teaspoon salt

1 cup warm water

1 package rapid rise yeast

1 teaspoon sugar

1 ½ Tablespoons olive oil

In a food processor mix flour and salt. In a 2-cup measuring cup add water, sugar, and yeast, stir to mix, and let it stand to bloom (bubble). Add yeast to the food processor. Drizzle with olive oil and mix until a ball of dough forms.

Grease a bowl with olive oil and place dough in bowl. Cover and set aside to rise.

NOTE: Do not put dough in an area where there is a draft or cool air. If necessary, put bowl in the microwave and let it rise quietly.

Punch it down and let it rise a second time.

Roll out or stretch into pizza pan of your choice. Top with your favorite toppings. Bake in a preheated 425° oven for 20 minutes.

Option:

Fried Pizza Dough

Heat ¼ cup vegetable oil to 350° in a deep edge frying pan. Cut off pieces of dough, stretch and fry. Fry on one side and turn to fry the other side. Serve with honey or sugar or cinnamon sugar.

BASIL ROASTED CHICKEN WITH GARLIC SAUCE

Heat oven to 400^0 and then 350^0

1- 3 ½ pound chickens (whole)

½ cube butter softened

4 teaspoons dried basil– crumbled

½ teaspoon salt

½ teaspoon pepper

1 cups fresh basil leaves (1 cup julienned)

40 cloves unpeeled garlic

½ cup dry white wine

1 can chicken broth

Preheat oven to 400^0. Wash chickens inside and out with water and pat dry with paper towel. Loosen breast skin with fingers. Mix ½ butter, dried basil, salt, and pepper in a bowl. Rub ½ the mixture under the skin and rub the remaining butter mixture over the chicken. Tuck ½ cup whole basil leaves under the skin. Place chickens in a roast pan and add garlic cloves to pan. Roast for 15 minutes then reduce heat to 350^0 and roast for another 15 minutes. Pour wine over chicken and baste with juices. Roast 15 minutes on each side basting with juices. Remove chicken from pan and cover with foil to keep warm. Pour pan juice and garlic into food processor. Add chicken broth and puree. Strain through sieve into saucepan. Boil to sauce consistency.

Serve sauce separately.

BOCCALINO'S CAESAR SALAD

This recipe was from Boccalino's restaurant in Denver. After shopping at a nearby mall, my friends and I would often end up at Boccalino's for Caesar Salad, which was always delightful. One day after many compliments, the chef arrived at our table and shared the recipe.

4 anchovy filets

Juice of half a lemon

½ teaspoon black pepper

½ teaspoon Dijon mustard

1 clove garlic mashed

1 teaspoon Worcestershire sauce

1 egg

1/3 cup extra virgin olive oil

1 head Romaine lettuce

1 Tablespoon Parmesan or Romano cheese

Croutons or Breadsticks

Dressing:

In a food processor: Add anchovies, lemon juice, mustard, pepper, garlic, Worcestershire sauce and egg. Mix and slowly drizzle olive oil to make an emulsion.

Tear lettuce in a bowl, pour dressing over and toss to coat. Sprinkle with cheese and add croutons.

Makes 4 servings.

BRACIOLE

Growing up on the farm, these delectable little bundles of stuffed steak were a staple. Mom would slice whatever cut of meat she had, stuff them with breadcrumbs, brown them, and toss them in red pasta sauce. She would cook them for a couple hours, tenderizing the meat. So good; time consuming, but worth the effort.

2 sirloin steaks sliced into thin strips

½ cup Romano cheese

1 cup Italian seasoned breadcrumbs

4 cloves garlic finely chopped

¼ cup fresh or dried parsley finely chopped

¼ cup fresh or dried basil leaves finely chopped

½ teaspoon salt

½ teaspoon pepper

Olive oil to brush meat

String to tie into meat bundles

Mix cheese, breadcrumbs, garlic, parsley, basil, salt, and pepper and set aside.

Pound slices of meat until thin.

Lay on cutting board and brush each slice of meat with oil – spread 1 teaspoon of crumb mixture down the middle of the meat and evenly spread out. Do not go all the way to the edge. Roll the strip and tie with string to hold ends closed. (You can also use a toothpick.) Repeat until all the meat is filled and rolled.

Brown in frying pan on all sides and transfer to pot of Tomato sauce to simmer for a minimum of 90 minutes.

Can be made a day ahead. Put meat bundles and sauce in fridge so the flavors can marry.

HOMEMADE QUICK BREAKFAST

Pancakes: Or as my Grandma Spano would say, "panny-cakes."

2 cups all-purpose flour

¼ cup sugar

4 teaspoons baking powder

¾ cup milk (or buttermilk)

½ teaspoon salt

1 egg

¼ stick melted butter

Mix flour, sugar, salt, and baking powder in a bowl and make a well. Add milk, egg, and butter, whisk until you have a smooth batter. If it is thick add more milk.

Butter a griddle or non-stick frying pan with butter and on medium heat pour batter into the desired size–little "silver dollar" cakes or regular big flap-jack cakes. Loosen edges with spatula after they start to bubble, turn (flip) and cook on the other side. Serve with syrup and more butter!

French Toast:

4 slices bread–your choice

½ cup milk

4 eggs

½ teaspoon vanilla

Whisk eggs, milk, and vanilla. Soak bread in mixture on both sides. Butter a griddle or non-stick frying pan and cook slices of bread until egg is browned. Serve warm with butter, sugar, or syrup.

CANNING DILL PICKLES

This is an easy recipe if you like homemade dill pickles. The men in my family would get involved in helping and then would enjoy the fruits of their labor!

Fill sink with cold water, add pickles and clean. Drain in colander.

Rinse wide mouth quart jars with boiling water.

Into each clean jar add:

¼ cup white vinegar

1 Tablespoon pickling salt

4 cloves of garlic (whole)

3 or four hot red peppers

3 or 4 rings of white onion slices

3 or 4 springs of fresh dill flowers on stem

Add the above amount of vinegar, pickling salt, garlic, hot peppers, onion slices and dill flowers into EACH jar. Line pickles into the jars until full. Pour boiling water in jar nearly to the top and seal lightly the jars with lids.

Place bottles in a large canning pan and boil 10 minutes in a hot water bath. Remove from water and let stand overnight until cold. Tighten the lids and store for 2 months BEFORE eating.

You will need proper canning tools to handle hot jars.

Eleanor Gaccetta

CANNING SWEET PICKLES

Rinse wide mouth quart jars.

Into each jar add:

1 cup white vinegar

½ teaspoon Alum

1 level Tablespoon salt

¾ Tablespoon pickling spice

Fill each jar with water, cap and let stand 3-4 weeks until ready to process.

To Process:

Rinse pickles in cold water and slice into a bowl.

For *each* quart you are canning add:

1 cup sugar and 1 ½ Tablespoon water

Stir until dissolved. Stir often for 24 hours. Add pickles to jars, refrigerate and enjoy.

CAPONATA

Every year during the late summer months the family would gather to make this relish which would be canned and eaten during the winter months. My grandmother would cook the eggplant over an open pit outdoors. The men would carry heavy pots and keep wood on the fire. My mother would cook celery in the oven. The kitchen would be a hub of activity for two days. ***This is a canning recipe that takes two days to prepare and yields 26 pints.***

This relish can be eaten alone, as a relish, condiment, or an accompaniment with chicken or beef.

7 Eggplants

6 stalks celery

1 gallon olive oil

1 commercial size can tomato puree, plus 1 can water

1-12 oz. can tomato paste, plus 1 can water

2 cups white vinegar

4-6 cups sugar

15 oz. capers, drained

1 cup dried basil leaves, crushed or crumbled

6 cups green olives chopped

3 cups pine nuts

Day 1:

Chop celery and cook in large roast pan in 350° oven until done. Stir frequently. Store in refrigerator overnight. Peel eggplant and cut into medium size cubes. Place in colander, salt liberally and drain overnight. **NOTE:** Place colander in pan or dishpan as the liquid will stain a sink.

Day 2:

In a ***large*** frying pan, heat 1 1/2 cups olive oil and fry eggplant in batches. In a ***very large*** sauce pot, add tomato puree, tomato paste, celery6, water, vinegar, sugar, capers, chopped olives, basil, and pine nuts. Stir to blend and let come to a boil over medium-high heat. Once all the eggplant is fried, add to sauce, and cook for an additional 15 minutes.

In a 3-quart saucepan add 3 inches of water and warm on medium heat. Place clean pink jars in the water bath upright. Pan may hold 4 or 5 at once.

Using canning tools, fill the jars with the eggplant mixture. Tightly close lids and place jars in a cool, dry place overnight to settle. Tighten lids. Jars can be stored for a year.

CHEESE PINEAPPLE SALAD

1 envelope unflavored gelatin

¼ cup cold water

¾ cup sugar

½ cup pineapple syrup

1 cup crushed pineapple drained

1 cup grated long horn cheese

1 cup cool whip

1-7 oz. can cranberry sauce thinly sliced

Soften gelatin in cold water. Dissolve sugar in pineapple syrup in saucepan over low heat. Add soften gelatin and stir until dissolved. Chill in refrigerator until mixture is consistency of syrup. Fold in pineapple, cheese, and cool whip. Pour into a ½ quart serving dish, garnish with cranberry cut-outs. Chill until firm.

Eleanor Gaccetta

CRAB BISQUE SOUP

1-10.75 oz. condensed cream of celery soup

1-12 oz. can evaporated milk

1-6 oz. can crab, drained and flaked

¼ teaspoon garlic powder

¼ teaspoon black pepper

Place all the ingredients in a saucepan and stir over medium heat. Bring to a boil and serve.

This soup can also be pureed if you want a creamed, smooth soup.

CRAB CAKES

1 cup seasoned breadcrumbs

2 green onions finely chopped

1 large egg eaten

¼ cup mayonnaise

1 Tablespoon lemon juice

½ teaspoon garlic powder

1/8 teaspoon cayenne pepper

2-6 oz cans crab meat

1 Tablespoon butter

In a bowl mix 1/3 cup breadcrumbs, green onions, egg, mayonnaise, lemon juice, garlic powder and cayenne pepper. Gently fold in crab.

Place remaining breadcrumbs in a bowl. Make 8-2-inch balls and gently roll in breadcrumbs and shape into 1/2-inch-thick patties. Heat butter in skillet over medium heat. Cook crab cakes 3 to 4 minutes on each side.

Eleanor Gaccetta

EASY SUNDAY POT ROAST

Sunday meals usually consisted of pasta, but occasionally in the winter, Mom would make pot roast. Crock pots were the latest and greatest cooking utensils, but she would also make this in a large roast pan and cook in the oven for several hours. This is a family dish.

Made in a Crock Pot

1 lbs. chuck roast, fat trimmed

1 small container sliced mushrooms

1 large onion, cut in half and then sliced

3 whole carrots cut into ½ inch pieces

2 bay leaves

1 can beef broth

1 Tablespoon black pepper

1 ½ teaspoon salt

In a large skillet add 1 Tablespoon oil and brown roast on all sides to seal in juices. This process takes about 10 minutes.

Put onions and carrots in the bottom of the crockpot. Pot the roast in with any juices from the frying pan. Add beef broth and mushrooms and seasonings. Make sure liquid nearly covers the roast – can add water or more broth.

Start crock pot on high for 45 minutes and then reduce to low and cook at least five hours.

MRS. OLQUIN'S ENCHILADAS

When I was a freshman in high school, I met the Olguin family. The five daughters became like family members and eventually our parents became friends. Five decades later our parents are deceased, and the sisters and I are still friends. These are what you call lasting friendships! In addition to great friendships, we also got to eat great Mexican food.

Preheat oven to 325^0

Filling:

1 lb. hamburger cooked and drained, or can use shredded, cooked chicken

1 lb. shredded sharp cheddar cheese

1 onion diced or small bunch of green onions cut (stems cut too)

Prepare filling and set aside in a bowl.

1 package corn tortillas – set aside

Sauce:

In a small saucepan:

Heat 2-3 Tablespoons vegetable oil add 2 Tablespoons chile powder, and Tablespoons all-purpose flour and stir to make a rue.

Add 2 ½ cups cold water and turn up heat to thicken sauce. Salt to taste and let simmer for 10 minutes.

To Assemble:

Dip corn tortillas in sauce to soften, place on a dish and repeat until all the tortillas are dipped and soft.

Fill each tortilla with filling, roll tightly and line in a 9 x 13 pan. When the dish is filled, pour remaining sauce over top and sprinkle with cheese and onions.

Bake 15-20 minutes until cheese melts.

Serve immediately. Can be frozen. Can be warmed in a microwave.

Eleanor Gaccetta

CRUSTY FISH STICKS FROM FRESH FISH

Why eat bought fish sticks when you can make your own healthy version?

Preheat oven to 425^0

Aioli – dipping sauce:

Whisk together, cover and chill:

½ cup mayonnaise

¼ cup finely chopped parsley or cilantro

1 clove garlic finely minced

¼ teaspoon cayenne pepper

1/8 teaspoon salt

Fish:

Place a cast iron skillet in 425^0 oven

12 oz. haddock or cod filets cut into 3 ¾ inch "sticks"

½ cup buttermilk

2 teaspoons bottled hot pepper sauce

¾ cup cornstarch

2 eggs

1 cup panko breadcrumbs

2 teaspoons dried parsley or cilantro

½ teaspoon garlic powder

½ cup olive oil

Salt and pepper to taste

Place fish in a large re-sealable bag. In a bowl, whisk together buttermilk, hot pepper sauce, salt, and pepper. Pour over fish to season and set aside.

In 3 shallow bowls:

1 – Mix cornstarch, 1/8 teaspoon salt and 1/8 teaspoon pepper

2 – Beat eggs

3 – Combine panko breadcrumbs, garlic powder, and ½ teaspoon salt

Discard marinade and drain fish. Gently dip fish sticks in cornstarch to coat, then into eggs and then coat with the panko mixture. Transfer to dish or tray.

Carefully remove skillet from oven and add ½ cup olive oil. Carefully arrange fish sticks in the pan. Bake 10 minutes and then turn fish and bake 8 additional minutes on other side.

Transfer fish to paper towels and let stand 5 minutes.

Serve with aioli. Serves 4.

GRANDMA SPANO'S EGGPLANT

This is a very rich, decadent dish. Our maternal grandmother would stuff and roll each slice of cooked eggplant and layer it a 9 x 13 pan. While caring for Mother, I would make this dish when my brother and sister-in-law would join us for Sunday dinner. We began layering eggplant to save time from rolling each slice. This dish is layers of eggplant, a breadcrumb mixture, and sauce. For smaller amounts, it can be made in a square cake pan or in a 9 x 13 Pyrex dish. Three regular eggplant or 5 Japanese eggplant are washed and either thinly sliced or cut into thin rounds.

Line cookie sheet with parchment paper and line eggplant close together (may need two cookie sheets). Roast eggplant for 30 minutes, turning once.

NOTE: Other option is to fry eggplants in vegetable oil and drain on paper towels.

Stuffing:

2 cups Italian seasoned breadcrumbs

1/2 cup Romano cheese

2 Tablespoons chopped parsley

2 Tablespoons chopped basil

3 cloves garlic finely chopped

Salt and pepper to taste

Combine all the stuffing ingredients in a bowl and set aside.

Sauce:

2-3 cloves garlic finely chopped

3 Tablespoons olive oil

1 large can tomato sauce + 1 small can tomato sauce + 2 small cans water

2 Tablespoons basil leaves

2 teaspoons salt

1 teaspoon pepper

1 Tablespoon sugar

1 Tablespoon white vinegar

In a saucepan sauté garlic in olive oil until slightly brown – do not burn; it will make the garlic bitter.

Add tomatoes and water, basil, salt, pepper, and sugar. Stir. The sauce should be slightly sweet. Bring to a boil, reduce heat and simmer for 30 minutes and add vinegar and simmer for another

20 minutes.

Preheat oven to 400⁰

Cover the bottom of your dish with sauce, cover sauce with a layer of eggplant and sprinkle stuffing liberally over eggplant. Repeat process of sauce, eggplant and stuffing until the dish is full. Top with layer of stuffing and sauce.

Bake in 400⁰ oven for 20 minutes to combine flavors and heat thoroughly. Let sit for 5 minutes and cut into squares. Serve as a side dish with meat, poultry, or pasta.

TRUE SOUTHERN FRIED CHICKEN

My Uncle Ray was born in Texas. This recipe was one of his favorites.

Marinade for chicken:

2 pounds chicken pieces – can be any part you like or whole chicken cut up.

2 cups buttermilk

Salt and Pepper to taste

1 teaspoon hot sauce

In a bowl combine chicken, buttermilk, salt, pepper, and hot sauce. Add chicken and make sure all pieces are covered in marinade. Set aside and refrigerate for at least 30 minutes.

Coating Mixture:

2 cups all-purpose flour

2 Tablespoons cornstarch

1 Tablespoon salt

½ Tablespoon pepper

2 teaspoons paprika

Vegetable, canola, or peanut oil to fry

Combine flour, cornstarch, salt, pepper, and paprika in a large bowl.

Heat oil to 350^0. You can use a deep fryer or frying pan. Discard the marinade. Dip each piece of chicken in the flour mixture to coat thoroughly. Dip in hot oil and fry until done. Cooking times vary for chicken parts, i.e. breasts need more cooking time than wings.

This is a messy dredging process.

GARLIC JAM

When making this recipe, make sure to have ample ventilation in the kitchen or house. I recommend NOT making it in the winter, as I did because you will be asphyxiated from garlic fumes! However, the result is a tasty condiment for pork or meat. But the process is smelly!

2 pounds cored and chopped apples

4 heads of garlic cloves crushed

8 cups water

2 cups sugar

1 ½ teaspoons lemon juice

In a large pot boil apples and garlic in water 45 minutes to 1 hour until soft.

Strain apples and garlic through a sieve. Set over bowl pressing on the solids to extract juices.

NOTE: I remove the apples and garlic using a slotted spoon. I puree them in a food processor with a few solids remaining.

Return to the pan, stir in sugar, and bring to a simmer. Simmer until the liquid is reduced – about 2 hours. Remove from the heat, stir in lemon juice. Chill before serving.

Makes 2 pints and can be stored in refrigerator for two months.

QUICK AMERICAN GREEN CHILE

2 – 3 pounds cubed pork

1 medium onion diced

1 jar medium spice picante sauce

1 can refried beans

½ cup Cold water

1 Tablespoon all-purpose flour

Salt and pepper to taste

2 teaspoon cumin

2 teaspoon chile powder

In a large saucepan cook pork until brown (may need to add 2 Tablespoons vegetable oil). Remove pork from the pan. To the pan add flour to make a rue and add ice water, stirring constantly and scraping the bottom of the pan. Return the pork to the pan and add remaining ingredients. Bring to a boil and reduce heat and allow to simmer for 30 minutes.

HOMEMADE CHICKEN SOUP

This was, and still is, a winter-time staple in our house. Nothing warms the soul like a bowl of homemade chicken soup.

4 chicken thighs (bone-in)

2 chicken breasts (can be either bone-in or boneless)

1 large onion finely diced

4 large carrots peeled and cut into small pieces or you can substitute ½ bag of petite baby carrots cut in half

3 ribs celery cut in small pieces (optional)

2 boxes reduced sodium chicken stock

1 cup water

1 Tablespoon parsley (fresh or dried)

1 teaspoon Better than Bouillon (chicken flavor)

1 cup cooked Ditalini pasta

In a large stock pot combine chicken, onion, carrots, parsley chicken stock and water. Cover and bring to a boil and turn down to a simmer and cook for one hour. Remove chicken from pan if you wish to remove meat from bones, shred or dice and return to pot. Add Better than Bouillon flavor and let simmer for another 45 minutes. Taste broth and if bland add salt and pepper to taste.

NOTE: Chicken can be left on bone – the marrow from the bone contains very nutritional properties.

I recommend cooking the pasta separately and set aside in a bowl with a little butter to keep from sticking. Add it to the soup just before serving. You may also cook pasta in the soup after you return chicken to the soup. Cooked pasta added to soup will absorb stock after the soup is cooked. Cooking pasta in the soup can make it starchy and the pasta overcooked.

Store leftover soup in refrigerator in an air-tight container. Great left-over dish.

ITALIAN BREADING FOR BEEF, OR LAMB

Growing up, my mother would occasionally bread steak for dinner. This is a beautiful and tasty way to serve meat. A breaded rack of baked lamb is so delectable. Try this for a real treat.

NOTE: This recipe is for 2 rib-eye steaks, 2 T-bone steaks, or 2- 6 oz. sirloin steaks.

Also, it can be for a small rack of lamb, 8 loin chops, or 2 lamb sirloin steaks.

1 ½ cups Seasoned Italian breadcrumbs

3 Tablespoons fresh or dried parsley chopped

2-3 cloves garlic finely chopped

Salt and pepper to taste

Olive oil to coat meat

Combine breadcrumbs, parsley, garlic, salt, and pepper in a bowl. Set aside. Rub both sides of meat with olive oil. Spray baking pan with non-stick spray. Coat both sides of meat generously in bread crumb mixture and place in baking sheet. Drizzle top of meat with olive oil before cooking.

Steak (beef) should be broiled. Cooking times will vary depending upon degree of doneness you desire and thickness of the meat.

Lamb should be baked at 350^0 for 20-30 minutes and allowed to rest 5 minutes before eating.

ITALIAN CHICKEN FINGERS

These little strips of chicken "tenders" are moist and a great quick dinner. They can be paired with most anything from potatoes to vegetables to salad.

1 package chicken cut into strips or a whole chicken breast cut into strips

2 large eggs

Salt and pepper

2 Tablespoon milk

2 teaspoons hot sauce

1 ½ cups all-purpose flour

½ cup Italian-seasoned breadcrumbs

½ teaspoon baking soda

½ teaspoon paprika

Salt and pepper to taste

Romano cheese (optional)

Vegetable oil for cooking

Mix eggs, salt and pepper, milk, and hot sauce in a bowl. Put chicken in a large zip-lock bag and pour wet mixture over and set aside to marinate for 20-30 minutes.

Heat vegetable oil to 350⁰.

Mix flour, breadcrumbs, baking soda, paprika, salt, pepper, and cheese in a deep dish. Dredge chicken in flour mixture and fry until done–generally 5 minutes on each side.

Chicken can be oven fried. Heat oven to 400⁰. Line cookie sheet with parchment paper. Line dredged chicken on pan and drizzle with oil. Bake 12-14 minutes, turning once.

ITALIAN PORK ROLLS

Pork is best used for making pasta sauce. These little rolls of deliciousness were often served as a baked side dish at Sunday dinner. I began making them as the main dish when Mom would ask for something light for dinner. I served them with a salad. Today, I make them as a main dish and serve them with Panzanella salad.

1 Pork loin roll (not more than 2 lbs.) partially frozen

2 cups Seasoned Italian breadcrumbs

3 Tablespoons fresh or dried parsley chopped

4 cloves garlic finely chopped

¼ cup Roman cheese

Salt and Pepper to taste

1/4-1/3 cup olive oil

Mix breadcrumbs, parsley, garlic, cheese, salt, and pepper in a bowl and set aside.

On a cutting board with a sharp knife–thinly slice pork loin.

With a kitchen mallet pound each strip into a long thin strip. Brush each strip with olive oil and put a ½ teaspoon breading mixture down the middle. Do not skimp–use more if needed.

Roll each strip and place seam side down on a baking dish sprayed with non-stick coating. Line closely together. Drizzle remaining oil over pork rolls–use more if needed. Cover with plastic wrap or foil and refrigerate for 1 hour.

Preheat oven to 350⁰. Bake for 20-30 minutes turning once.

The rolls can also be stacked on skewers and cooked on a cookie sheet sprayed with non-stick spray.

LINGUINE WITH CLAM SAUCE

This is a variation of traditional Linguine with Clam Sauce, as it includes 3 cups of tomato sauce.

Father David, the family priest, would sometimes accept Mon's invitation for dinner. This recipe was one of his favorites. I cooked this at his request. My nieces would say it was a lot of work for it not even being a dinner date!

Tomato Sauce:

1 small can crushed tomatoes + 1 can water

1 Tablespoon olive oil

1 clove garlic finely chopped

2 teaspoons sugar

Salt and pepper to taste

Sauté garlic in olive oil, add tomatoes, water, sugar, salt, and pepper and bring to a boil. Reduce to a simmer and cook for 45 minutes. Set aside.

Clam Sauce:

½ cup olive oil

3 cloves garlic sliced

½ shallot finely chopped

¼ teaspoon red pepper flakes

3 pounds little neck clams

1 cup dry white wine

¼ cup chopped parsley

½ teaspoon salt

½ teaspoon pepper

½ teaspoon basil

1 ½ pounds cooked Linguine pasta

Toasted Italian seasoned breadcrumbs

Loaf of crusty bread

In a large saucepan or sauté pan heat olive oil, add garlic and shallots and cook for 2 minutes. Add crushed red pepper and clams to coat clams. Add wine and cook, reducing heat slightly. Add 3 cups of tomato sauce and cover pan and cook until clams open – about 10 minutes.

Uncover and remove any clams that are not opened. Add parsley, salt, pepper, basil and stir. Add cooked pasta and pour into a large bowl. Can be topped with toasted breadcrumbs or Romano cheese.

Serve with crusty bread.

MANDARIN SALAD

Salad:

1/4 cup slivered almonds

1 large can mandarin oranges – drained

1/2 head Romaine lettuce, cut

2-3 ribs celery chopped

3 green onions chopped

Dressing:

Mix:

1/3 cup olive oil

1/4 cup seasoned rice vinegar

1 Tablespoon sugar

1 teaspoon dried or fresh parsley

1/4 teaspoon red pepper flakes

Salt and pepper to taste

Add salad ingredients into a bowl and add mixed dressing and toss.

Eleanor Gaccetta

OMAHA WHITE CHILE

This is a great variation of chile for a winter evening. My late sister-in-law, Connie, shared this recipe with me while I was providing 24/7 care to Mom. It was a great meal to prepare if friends were coming over to see Mom and staying for dinner. This can be made in a crock pot or in a large soup pot on the stove.

1 Chicken breast cooked and shredded (Substitute shredded store bought rotisserie chicken, or 3 small cans of chicken)

3 cups White Northern beans

1 can Rotele chiles/tomatoes

1 Tablespoon olive oil

1 medium onion – diced

3 cloves garlic chopped

1 cup diced green chiles

2 teaspoons cumin

1 teaspoon oregano

1 teaspoon cayenne pepper

1 Tablespoon salt

1-14 oz. box chicken stock

3 cups grated Monterrey Jack cheese

1 medium carton sour cream

In a large chile pot or crock pot combine broth and chicken.

In a skillet on medium heat add olive oil, onion, garlic, chiles, cumin, oregano, salt, and pepper and sauté until the onions are translucent. Add to chicken and simmer for 1 hour.

Before serving add cheese and sour cream to taste individually.

PANZANELLA SALAD

Italian Bread Salad

This is a family favorite. The crusty bread soaked in a sweet vinaigrette loaded with little bites of vegetables is filling and a treat to the palate. This can be a salad or main dish.

Vinaigrette:

In a medium to large bowl make the vinaigrette, stir, and set aside:

½ cup olive oil

¼ cup seasoned Rice vinegar

¼ cup Red Wine vinegar

½ teaspoon salt

2 cloves minced garlic

Red pepper flakes (to taste)

Croutons:

Cube a loaf of crusty Artisan bread. Add 2 Tablespoons olive oil to a frying pan. On low to medium heat toss the bread until dry and edges are brown (about 10 minutes).

This salad can be made with any vegetable cut into small pieces. You can also add chunks of ham, cheese, or salami for more of a main dish.

My favorite vegetables to use are:

½ diced red onion

½ carton cherry tomatoes cut in half

1 cucumber peeled and diced

1 red pepper cut into thin slices

1 yellow pepper cut into thin slices

1 small stock broccoli florets trimmed

1-2 ribs celery finely chopped

Add toasted bread to vinaigrette and toss to coat. Add vegetables and stir to coat evenly. Cover with plastic wrap and refrigerate for 2 hours before serving.

HOMEMADE PASTA

Growing up, Grandma Spano would put flour on a big wooden board, make a well, and add eggs, a pinch of salt, and water. She would diligently work the flour, never spilling anything. Soon she would knead and work the dough with her hands and produce a gorgeous ball of pasta dough. Today, pasta can be made in a mixer with a dough hook or in a food processor. A pasta machine or pasta attachment to a mixer can also be used. There is nothing like the taste of homemade pasta.

The rule of thumb for making homemade pasta is to use:

1 cup all-purpose flour–you can use semolina flour as well.
1 egg
1 pinch of salt
Water to moisten–teaspoon of olive oil
Pasta for two people:
2 cups all-purpose flour,
2 eggs,
¼ teaspoon salt,
water (close to ¼ cup)
1 Tablespoon olive oil

Put ingredients in a food processor and pulse until dough forms a ball. On a floured surface knead the dough by hand until it is smooth and a soft texture.

Slice pasta into thin rounds, flatten with hands and coat with all-purpose flour. Roll through the pasta machine, coat with flour and roll through the pasta cutter. Repeat for each round of dough.

Uncooked pasta can be frozen on a cookie tray fresh and then transferred to a plastic bag and stored in the freezer.

To cook pasta:

Bring a pot of water to boil–add a Tablespoon of salt to the water. Cook fresh pasta for 3minutes and cook frozen pasta for 5 minutes. Drain thoroughly in a colander and serve with your choice of sauce.

PASTA WITH CHEESE AND PEPPER

Fill large pan with water and 2 Tablespoons salt and set to boil 1 lb. Pasta–Angel Hair, Bucatini, Spaghetti, etc.

Cook pasta according to instructions. While pasta is cooking, make sauce.

Sauce:

¼ cup olive oil

2 Tablespoons butter

2 cloves garlic finely chopped

2 teaspoons black pepper

1 Tablespoon fresh parsley chopped

¾ cup water

4 oz. Romano cheese

Heal olive oil and butter in large frying pan over medium heat. Add garlic and pepper and sauté for about 35 seconds. Remove from heat, add ¾ cup water, return to heat, and bring to boil.

Drain pasta and add to sauce. Toss and sprinkle with cheese. Can add more liquid as needed. Top with additional cheese and pepper to taste.

PASTA FISHERMAN STYLE

This is a favorite from Scoma's on the Wharf, a restaurant in San Francisco, California. After visiting San Francisco several times, I sometimes made this dish for company, but mostly I made it for Mom and me. Mom loved fish and this is a beautiful dish.

1 large can crushed tomatoes

1 medium onion finely diced

3 Tablespoons olive oil + 2 Tablespoons for mushrooms

2 cloves garlic minced

1 small carton Baby Bella mushrooms, chopped

2 1/2 teaspoons salt

2 1/2 teaspoon black pepper

2 teaspoons dried basil–crushed

2 1/2 teaspoon dried parsley crushed

1 Tablespoon sugar

1 package vacuum packed crab (found in fresh fish section of grocery store)

In a non-stick frying pan, sauté mushrooms in 2 Tablespoons olive oil, add 1 teaspoon each salt, pepper, and parsley, and 1 clove of minced garlic. Cook until mushrooms are soft. Put in bowl and set aside.

In a saucepan pan, sauté onions and remaining garlic in 3 Tablespoons olive oil until translucent. Add tomatoes, remaining salt, pepper, parsley, basil, and sugar. Bring to a boil and let simmer 15 minutes. Add mushrooms and crab and simmer 30 minutes.

Cook any variety pasta, drain, and add to sauce.

Eleanor Gaccetta

PASTA WITH LENTILS

This was a winter-time favorite growing up. Mom would make a big pot of pasta with lentils and it would warm every inch of your soul. It is not a difficult dish to make and we enjoyed it regularly until she passed away.

6 Tablespoons olive oil

1 large onion finely diced

¾ teaspoon salt

¼ teaspoon pepper

1-12 oz. can diced tomatoes

½ cup Red lentils

2 cups water

¾ pound medium shell pasta

In a large saucepan sauté onion in olive oil until translucent. Add salt, pepper, and tomatoes. Stir in lentils and water. Simmer for 20-25 minutes until lentils are soft. Cooking time may vary as some variety of lentils take longer to cook. Add water as needed to keep lentils covered in liquid.

Cook pasta according to package, drain and add to lentils. Serve with cheese.

PASTA WITH OLIVE OIL AND GARLIC

This dish is a staple in most Italian families. It is a dish that you can quickly prepare when company unexpectedly shows up. Pair it with a salad and you have a lovely meal. I remember my grandmother making this when time was short; and on the farm, I remember my mother taking all the time in the world. I make it often.

1/2 pound Angel Hair pasta

1/3 cup olive oil

2 Tablespoons butter

2 cloves garlic, finely minced

1/2 teaspoon red pepper flakes

1 Tablespoon chopped parsley for serving

Romano cheese for serving

Place a cold frying pan on medium heat and warm the olive oil and melt the butter. Add garlic and sauté and add red pepper flakes. Add pasta water and simmer so the water boils out, but the starch remains.

Bring a large pot of salted water to boil and add pasta to cook. Add a ¼ cup pasta water to the olive oil mixture, drain cooked pasta. Add to olive oil and toss to coat all the pasta.

Place in a serving bowl and sprinkle liberally with cheese.

PASTA SALAD

Looking for a summertime side dish for a barbeque or picnic? This is quick and can be made ahead of time and stored in the refrigerator. My niece, Pam, started bringing pasta salads to family gatherings at my brother's house. The big bowl would be empty by the end of the gathering. Unlike potato salad or macaroni salad, this dish does not have mayonnaise and does not need to be kept cold during hot weather.

1 package tri-colored Rotini pasta cooked and drained

1 can chopped olives, drained

8 oz. package grape tomatoes

4 ribs celery chopped

½ red onion finely diced, or green onions chopped

1 cucumber seeded and sliced

½ package mini-pepperoni slices

1 small package cheese cubes or chop fresh mozzarella balls

Combine all the ingredients in a large bowl. You can use bottled Italian dressing or make the recipe below:

Dressing:

½ cup olive oil

¼ cup seasoned rice vinegar

1 teaspoon salt

1 teaspoon black pepper

¼ teaspoon red pepper flakes

Whisk together in a bowl and pour over salad. Toss, cover, and chill for 2-3 hours.

PASTA WITH PEAS AND HAMBURGER

This dish was always served at our Fourth of July family picnic. A big bowl was set on the table as a side dish and served with fried chicken or even hamburgers and hot dogs. Do not be fooled by the Fourth of July; it is a warm, comforting main dish in winter as well.

1-pound pasta–medium Shells, Farfalle, Rotini, or other small pasta. Cook, drain, and set aside in a bowl. Drizzle with olive oil and stir so it will not stick.

Hamburger Mixture:

1 lb. ground round or chuck beef at least 80-20

½ cup seasoned breadcrumbs

¼ cup Romano cheese (optional)

1 ½ teaspoon salt

1 teaspoon pepper

1 small onion finely diced

1 egg beaten

1 Tablespoon milk

2 Tablespoons chopped parsley, dried or fresh

In a bowl combine all the ingredients and mix thoroughly.

In a large saucepan add 2 Tablespoons olive oil.

Add hamburger mixture. Stir constantly over medium to medium-high heat until brown and crumbled. Add in 2 cloves garlic finely minced and brown.

Sauce:

1-12 1/2 oz. can crushed tomatoes

1-12 ½ oz. can tomato puree

1 can water

2 ½ teaspoons salt

2 teaspoons pepper

½ teaspoon crushed red pepper

1 ½ teaspoon basil, fresh or dried

1 Tablespoon sugar

¼ teaspoon garlic powder

½ small package frozen petite peas

Pour tomatoes and water over hamburger mixture. Add salt, pepper, red pepper, basil, sugar, and garlic powder and bring to a boil. Reduce heat and simmer 20 minutes, add peas and simmer 25 minutes. Stir frequently scraping the bottom of the pan to avoid sticking. Taste – sauce should be slightly sweet.

Add cooked, drained pasta to sauce, stir. Pour into a large bowl and serve with Romano cheese.

BASIL PESTO

Basil is harvested in the fall. It can be dried or frozen for use in winter cooking. We made large batches of pesto and stored it in the freezer for winter recipes. This recipe can be doubled.

Options for freezing:

Many ways to freeze include:

1: Fill empty ice cube trays with 1 Tablespoon pesto and top with a bit of butter – freeze.

2: Line a cookie sheet with parchment or waxed paper. Spoon 1 Tablespoon pesto in even intervals on the sheet–freeze.

Once frozen, pesto can be transferred to a plastic zip-lock bag for storage in the freezer. Whenever you make sauce or a dish with pesto just thaw before using.

2 cups fresh basil packed

2 cloves garlic

¼ cup pine nuts

¾ cup olive oil

½ cup Romano cheese

Pepper to taste

Butter (if freezing)

Put basil, garlic, nuts, cheese, and pepper in a food processer. Drizzle oil as the bowl blends. Judge after ½ cup oil if more is needed.

For pasta: cook and drain pasta, reserving ½ cup liquid. Add ¼ - ½ cube butter to the hot pasta then toss with pesto.

Eleanor Gaccetta

POLENTA

Polenta is an old-fashioned staple in Italy. Growing up my grandmother often cooked polenta (corn meal) in place of pasta. My mother would often cook it on Fridays during the time when Catholics were not allowed to eat meat.

Basic rule of thumb:

5 cups liquid to 1 cup dry polenta

5 cups liquid—can be a combination of water with milk or with chicken stock

1 Tablespoon salt

1 cup polenta

2 Tablespoons butter

½ cup Romano cheese

Bring 5 cups liquid to a rolling boil. Slowly add corn meal and salt stirring constantly. Reduce heat to low and stir for 3 to 5 minutes until creamy. Add butter and cheese.

Serve with pasta sauce.

NOTE: My family preference is to use finely ground corn meal (polenta) from an Italian specialty market. Coarse corn meal from a grocery store results in a dry dish and makes it difficult to achieve a creamy texture.

ITALIAN POTATO SALAD

This is a favorite any season of the year. It is a great addition to a summertime picnic since it does not have to remain cold or over ice like mayonnaise-based potato salads do.

1 lbs. red potatoes peeled and cut into 1 ½ inch cubes

1/3 cup olive oil

3 cloves garlic finely minced

1 teaspoon salt

1 teaspoon pepper

1 teaspoon red pepper flakes

1/4 cup seasoned Rice wine vinegar

Fresh chopped parsley for garnish

Cook potatoes until tender–about 15-20 minutes. Drain and place in a large bowl. Set aside.

In a skillet add olive oil, garlic, salt, and pepper and sauté for 1 minute or slightly more. Pour over potatoes, add vinegar, and gently stir to coat all the potatoes. Garnish with fresh parsley.

Eleanor Gaccetta

AMERICAN POTATO SALAD

This is my mom's version of American potato salad. She would make this often in the summer when vegetables were plentiful. You will notice it has a few twists and turns; she was good at improvising until the taste suited her.

2 lbs. Russet potatoes, cooked, skinned, drained and cubed

6 eggs hard boiled, cooled, peeled, and chopped

5 ribs celery finely diced

1 medium bunch green onions washed and cut, including green stems

½ cup sweet pickle relish

¼ teaspoon garlic salt

1 Tablespoon prepared yellow mustard

½ teaspoon celery salt

1 Tablespoon salt

Ground black pepper to taste

1 cup Miracle Whip Salad Dressing

Combine all the ingredients in a large bowl. Mix thoroughly to coat the ingredients evenly.

Chill in refrigerator.

PARTY PUNCH

Growing up there was always a family gathering of some sort to attend. Baptisms, first communions, confirmations, graduations, weddings, and baby showers were just a few of some we enjoyed. The ladies would always plan a buffet dinner or have trays of sweets. I am not even sure if there is such a thing as a punch bowl today. Today, see a cooler or bucket filled with ice and cans of soft drinks or bottles of various hard drinks. This is a refreshing drink that I remember making and drinking.

2 bottles of Ginger Ale or 7Up

1 large can frozen lemonade concentrate

1 large can frozen orange juice concentrate

Water

Ice

Make the lemonade and orange juice according to the instructions on the can. In a punch bowl, combine these with the soda. Add ice, stir, and enjoy.

If you want to make this an adult drink, add Vodka.

QUICHE LORRAINE

This is the perfect dish for Easter Brunch. When we were invited out for Easter brunch, mom would make two of these to contribute to the meal.

Preheat oven to 400°

One pie crust–can be homemade or store brought

4 to 5 strips bacon cooked crisp and crumbled

1 ½ cups cheddar and swiss cheese

½ medium onion finely chopped

½ small carton white button mushrooms chopped

3eggs

¾ cup half and half

½ teaspoon salt

½ teaspoon pepper

¼ teaspoon ground nutmeg

Prepare pie dough or unroll premade dough into a pie dish or quiche pan. Sprinkle cheese, bacon, onions, and mushrooms in the pie crust.

In a medium bowl whip eggs, half and half, salt, pepper, and nutmeg. Beat until mixed and pour over ingredients in the pie crust.

Bake 50-55 minutes until a knife inserted in the middle comes out clean. Let stand 10 minutes before serving.

RED CHILE

This is traditional chile con carne; not the Mexican version of green chile.

1 lb. ground beef (at least 80% lean)

1 large onion diced

2 cloves garlic chopped or ¼ teaspoon garlic powder

2 teaspoons dried oregano

1 teaspoon cumin

1 teaspoon chile powder

1 teaspoon salt

½ teaspoon red pepper sauce

14 oz. can diced tomatoes

1-15 oz. can red kidney beans drained

In a 3-quart saucepan, cook beef, onion, and chopped garlic until beef is cooked, stirring occasionally. Drain and return to pan. Stir in oregano, cumin, chile powder, salt, and tomatoes with all the liquid.

Cook 1 hour on low heat stirring occasionally. Add beans, bring to a boil, and reduce heat for another 20 minutes.

HOMEMADE RICOTTA CHEESE

This recipe is from my mother's cousin, Mary Balistreri. After Mary shared her recipe and the art of making homemade ricotta, Mom made this cheese often. It is creamy and delicious and unlike anything you can buy in a store. They would make it for holidays when the menu included raviolis.

2 quarts (1/2 gallon) Whole milk

1 quart of half and half

1/3 cup white vinegar

1 heaping Tablespoon salt

In a large pot on low to medium heat bring milk and half and half to a boil. This is a dish that requires patience because milk will take more than 30 minutes to boil. Stir frequently so milk does not stick (burn) on the bottom of the pan. Recommend using a wooden spoon.

Just as the milk begins to boil add vinegar and salt and stir. Once the milk begins to curdle remove from heat and use a slotted spoon or wire spatula to remove cheese into a colander lined with cheesecloth. Do not drain water.

Put pan with water (whey) back on heat and let it come to a boil and add another round of salt and vinegar. As the milk begins to curdle repeat the process to remove from heat and remove from the pan.

Drain the cheese. Store covered in the refrigerator. Use within 2 or 3 days. This will net approximately 2 ½ pounds of cheese.

RICOTTA GNOCCHI

Gnocchi is generally made from boiled, riced potatoes. My mother always thought they were too heavy a pasta and she declined to make and cook them. This recipe was created after eating Jewish matzo balls in chicken soup. Ricotta makes the gnocchi light, and this is best served with a lighter, simple sauce possibly one including vegetables.

1-16 oz. container ricotta cheese drained

2 cups flour (may need a bit more)

1 egg yolk

½ teaspoon salt

1 teaspoon each fresh chopped parsley and basil (optional)

In a mixing bowl add all the ingredients and mix until incorporated into a soft ball of dough. On a lightly floured surface roll the dough into a cylinder about 1 inch in diameter. Cut into 1 inch rounds.

Bring a pan of salted water to boil and carefully drop the gnocchi into the water. Cook for 5 minutes, drain, and enjoy. Add Romano cheese to serve.

CREAMY RICOTTA PASTA WITH SPINACH

8 oz. Angel Hair pasta

2 Tablespoons olive oil

1/3 cup roasted, chopped pistachio nuts

1 clove garlic minced

1 cup ricotta cheese

¼ teaspoon salt

½ cup grated Romano cheese

5 oz. spinach

Black pepper to taste

In a large pot of salted water, cook pasta.

In a large skillet, heat oil over medium-medium high heat. Add pistachios and garlic and sauté for 2 minutes. Stir in ricotta, salt, and ¼ cup pasta water until smooth. Stir in cheese. Add 1 cup pasta water and drain pasta. Put in sauce and add spinach. Gently toss and top with pepper and additional Romano cheese and pistachios.

ROASTED RED PEPPER DIP

This sort of just showed up as a variation for a dip to serve with chips or vegetables at a regular winter family gathering, generally known as Bronco Sunday.

1 package Knorr Tomato and Basil Soup Mix

1 ½ cups sour cream

½ cup mayonnaise

½ cup roasted red peppers

Mix soup mix, sour cream, and mayonnaise until smooth. Add pepper. Cover and chill for 2 hours.

NOTE: Pepper can be fresh roasted or jar roasted pepper (drained).

ST. LUCY DAY RICE BALLS

The Feast of St. Lucy (patron saint of eyes) is December 13th. Growing up it was a day for celebrating with a dinner of polenta and rice balls. Mom and her sisters would gather at our home and make dozens of rice balls for each to take back home for their dinners. Today my generation does not celebrate the day as our ancestors did, but on occasion we still make rice balls. The past few years my family has made them when we gathered to make Christmas cookies.

Sauce:

1 lb. ground beef

1 lb. ground pork

2 eggs

2 Tablespoons chopped parsley

Salt and pepper to taste (at least a teaspoon of each)

½ teaspoon red pepper flakes

¼ cup Romano cheese

1/3 cup Italian seasoned breadcrumbs

½ small onion finely diced

In a large bowl mix all the ingredients thoroughly. In a large saucepan fry in 3 Tablespoons of olive oil, stirring constantly to make a crumbly mixture.

When almost cooked add:

2 cloves garlic finely chopped

1 large can crushed tomatoes

½ can water

1 Tablespoon sugar

1 Tablespoon dried basil

Bring to a boil and reduce to a simmer stirring often for at least an hour.

Cook 2 -3 cups Japanese sticky rice per instructions on package. Cool in a large bowl.

Remove meat from sauce to a separate bowl.

To the rice add: ½ to ¾ cup pasta sauce, 2 egg yolks and 1 teaspoon cinnamon, stir to mix.

Heat oil for deep frying to 350⁰.

To make rice balls:

Place small amount of rice in palm of hand and form half a ball. Make an indentation and add 1- ½ teaspoon meat mixture. Cover with more rice and form a ball. Set aside on a cookie sheet and repeat until all the rice mixture is used.

In a bowl add:

2 cups Italian seasoned breadcrumbs

In a separate bowl add:

2 cups Cinnamon-Sugar (2 cups sugar and 1 Tablespoon cinnamon)

Roll balls in seasoned breadcrumbs and fry until brown, drain on paper towel and roll in cinnamon sugar. Place on a dish or tray.

SPICY GLAZED PECANS

This is a great snack to have on hand during the holidays. This snack can be made with most type of nuts.

Preheat Oven to 350⁰

1/3 cup sugar

3 Tablespoons water

½ teaspoon salt

1/2 teaspoon cayenne pepper

2 cups pecan halves

Butter for coating pan

Line a large, heavy baking sheet with parchment paper and coat with butter and set aside.

In a saucepan combine sugar, water, salt, and cayenne pepper. Stir over medium heat until sugar dissolves. Boil 2 minutes. Add nuts and stir until all are coated.

Transfer nuts to baking sheet and spread evenly. Bake until nuts turn brown.

Transfer cooked nuts to wax-paper-lined cookie sheet and separate with a fork.

Must work fast.

ITALIAN SPINACH – SIDE DISH

Everybody hates cooked spinach–the green vegetable that is only good in a salad. My mother created this dish when we were growing up on the farm. It is a wonderful side dish to beef, pork, chicken, or fish.

In a large skillet on medium heat add:

2 Tablespoons olive oil

1 small sack of spinach leaves washed, and stems removed

3 cloves of garlic finely chopped

½ teaspoon salt

½ teaspoon red pepper flakes

Constantly turn spinach as leaves wilt to ensure all the ingredients are mixed and the spinach is wilted and cooked.

Add ¼ cup Italian seasoned breadcrumbs to wilted spinach mixture. Turn off heat, cover, and let steam. Stir breadcrumbs into spinach.

Transfer to plate and enjoy while hot.

SPINACH SAUSAGE QUICHE

1 pie crust–can be store bought or homemade

8 oz. package bulk Italian sausage cooked and crumbled

½ cup onion chopped

1 clove garlic minced

¾ cup spinach drained and chopped

½ cup herb seasoned stuffing mix

1 ½ cups Swiss or Jack cheese, shredded

3 eggs

2/3 cup half and half

½ teaspoon Paprika

Put crust in pie pan or quiche pan, set aside.

Cook sausage and remove from pan to drain on paper towels.

Sauté onion and garlic, add spinach, stuffing mix and return sausage to pan.

Sprinkle cheese in the pie crust and add sausage mixture. In a bowl beat eggs, half and half, and paprika. Pour over pie pan. Bake 30-40 minutes or until toothpick inserted in middle comes out clean.

Cool 10 minutes before serving.

STEAMED DUMPLINGS

Growing up, Mom would make dumplings with chicken, soups, or stews in place of noodles. Generally, I make chicken and dumplings, but they are also great with soup. This is a hearty addition to any soup and not for the calorie conscious.

1 cup all-purpose flour

1 ½ teaspoons baking powder

½ teaspoon salt

1 egg beaten

½ cup milk

2 Tablespoons melted butter

Sift flour, baking powder and salt together. Combine egg, milk, and butter and add to dry ingredients. Drop from a teaspoon on top of liquid in soup or stew. Pan should have at least 3 quarts liquid. (If not, add boiling water). Cover pan and steam for 15 minutes.

STUFFED ARTICHOKES

This is a Sicilian dish from my mother's mother. Artichokes were served for Easter and fall holidays. Whenever my mother saw good artichokes, she bought and stuffed them. This is truly a specialty dish. It is sometimes served as a side dish, but it is hearty enough to enjoy as a meal. The availability of good artichokes then was limited to Easter and the fall months. Today artichokes are available year-round. Look for round artichokes and not those with pointed tips as they do not work well for this recipe.

NOTE: My mother always cooked artichokes in a pressure cooker for 25 minutes. Family members who were afraid of pressure cookers instead would clean and trim the outer leaves and cut the top and stem off and boil the artichokes for 30 minutes. They would then remove them from the water and dunk them into an ice bath. Then dry them, add stuffing, and bake at 325° for 2 hours, adding liquid, as necessary. Why am I mentioning this? Because it is important to determine which cooking method you will use before going to the effort of making this dish.

2 large round artichokes

2 large lemons

1 cup Italian seasoned breadcrumbs

2 garlic cloves finely minced

2 teaspoon parsley

Salt and pepper to taste

Anchovy filets chopped (optional)

Olive oil

Mix breadcrumbs, garlic, parsley, salt, and pepper, (anchovies) in a bowl and set aside.

Fill a dishpan or large bowl with cold water, cut one lemon in half, squeeze juice in the water and put the skin in the water as well. On a large tray using a sharp knife cut off the top of the artichoke about ¼ inch from the top. Trim the tips from the outer leaves with a kitchen scissor. Using your fingers, spread the artichoke open to make room for stuffing. Put the artichoke in the water open side down and repeat with other artichokes. Tap the water from artichoke.

NOTE: If you are using the boil and bake method to cook, this is where you put the artichokes in a pan of boiling water for 30 minutes and then place them in an ice bath.

Open the outer leaves and using a spoon, sprinkle breadcrumb mixture liberally inside the artichoke and in the outer leaf openings. Put in pan and drizzle tops with olive oil and drizzle a bit in the pan. Add water to the pan and cook. Bake for 2 hours adding water, as necessary.

Or put in a pressure cooker for 25 minutes.

SAUTÉED MUSHROOMS AND STUFFED MUSHROOMS

Sautéed Mushrooms:

1 package mushroom pieces or whole mushrooms chopped

2 Tablespoons olive oil

Salt and pepper to taste

¼ teaspoon red pepper flakes

2 cloves garlic finely minced

2 teaspoons parsley chopped

In a pan mix all the ingredients and fry until mushrooms are tender– about 10 minutes. Stir frequently. This is a wonderful quick and easy side dish.

Stuffed Mushrooms:

Preheat oven to 400⁰

28 large mushrooms, stems removed

½ cup Italian seasoned breadcrumbs

½ cup Romano cheese grated

2 cloves garlic finely minced

2 Tablespoons chopped parsley

Salt and pepper to taste

1/3 cup olive oil

½ lb. bulk sausage fried, crumbled, and drained

Mix all the ingredients in a bowl. Spoon mixture into each mushroom cavity. Drizzle tops with olive oil. Drizzle oil over baking sheet and line mushrooms evenly. Bake 25 minutes.

TOMATO, ARTICHOKE AND BASIL PASTA

1 Tablespoon salt

1 lb. pasta–your choice

3 Tablespoons olive oil

3 cloves garlic chopped

1 pint cherry tomatoes, rinsed and dried

½ jar quartered artichoke hearts with some liquid

8 oz. fresh mozzarella cheese balls cut in half

½ cup shredded fresh basil

Salt and pepper

Fill a large pot with water, add salt, bring to a boil, and cook pasta.

In a large skillet heat olive oil and sauté garlic. Add tomatoes, cook 5 minutes. Add artichokes and liquid and cook another 5 minutes.

Drain pasta and add to sauce, toss. Add basil and mozzarella cheese. Season with salt and pepper. Optional: add red pepper flakes.

Serves 4

TURKEY TETRAZZINI

(From left-over turkey)

This is a hearty dish that can be made from left-over turkey after Thanksgiving or on any chilly day.

Preheat oven to 400°

½ lb. pasta shells or tubes cooked and drained

5 Tablespoons butter

1 Tablespoon minced onion

½ lb. fresh mushrooms chopped

¼ cup all-purpose flour

2 cups milk (can use 2% or low fat)

½ teaspoon salt

¼ teaspoon pepper

2/3 cup Romano cheese

½ cup Italian seasoned breadcrumbs

3 cups chopped–cooked turkey

Cook pasta, drain, and set aside. In a large skillet melt 2 Tablespoons of butter and brown onion. Add mushrooms and cook 10 minutes stirring frequently. Sprinkle on flour and cook 1 minute, stirring constantly. Add milk, salt and pepper and stir until thick. Remove from heat and add cheese.

Spray a 3-quart baking dish with non-stick spray. Combine pasta with half the sauce. Stir turkey into remaining sauce and pour over pasta. Sprinkle with breadcrumbs and cheese. Top with remaining butter cut into pieces. Bake 20 minutes.

TUSCAN WHITE BEAN CHICKEN SOUP

1 lb. chicken breast

2 boxes reduced fat chicken stock

1 ½ cans cannellini beans

1 cup chopped yellow onion

1 cup chopped carrots

½ can diced tomatoes

½ teaspoon salt

½ teaspoon pepper

1- 2-inch cheese rind (optional) can be Parmesan, Parrano, or Romano

2 cups spinach leaves

Put chicken in stock pot with chicken stock and boil for about 20 minutes until cooked. (Can add water if more liquid is needed.) Remove chicken and shred or cut into small pieces. Return to the pot and add beans, carrots, onion, tomatoes, salt, pepper, and cheese rind. Simmer for 1 to 1 ½ hours. Add spinach and stir. May need to add water during the cooking process.

I like to add ½ teaspoon of Chicken Flavor Better than Bouillon for depth of flavor.

WHOLE BAKED CHICKEN

Baked chicken is healthy and nutritious. Today the modern family just buys a rotisserie chicken which is ready to take home and enjoy. This is an easy recipe and a sure way to impress upon your loved ones that you do know how to turn on the oven and use it!

Preheat oven to 400^0

1 Whole chicken (at least 2.5 pounds)

2 Tablespoons olive oil

2 teaspoons each salt, pepper, and garlic powder combined in a small bowl

Clean the chicken inside and out and dry. Place on a rack in a roasting pan.

Rub the skin of the entire chicken liberally with olive oil. Season chicken liberally putting some inside the cavity. Put ½ cup water in bottom of pan. Cover and bake for 30 minutes and uncover and cook for an additional 30 minutes. Skin will be crispy, and meat will be tender.

VEGETARIAN SANDWICH FOR ONE

2 slices Artisan bread

2 Roasted red peppers from jar

½ Avocado—sliced or smashed

Olive oil

1 Garlic clove cut in half

Salt

Pepper

1 large Portobella mushroom cap sautéed

Sauté mushroom cap whole in small amount of olive oil until soft. This can also be grilled or roasted in a 400° oven for 20 minutes.

Toast bread slices and rub with garlic clove, drizzle (brush) with olive oil. Spread avocado slices evenly on each slice of bread, top with salt and pepper. On one slice of bread add red pepper and sautéed mushroom cap. Top with other slice of bread and enjoy.

YUMMY ROASTED POTATOES

Preheat oven to 400^0

1 ½ lb. Red potatoes–peeled and quartered if small or wedged if large

2 Tablespoons olive oil

5 garlic cloves minced

½ tsp oregano

1/3 cup grated Parmesan or Roman cheese

Salt and pepper to taste

Line bottom of a baking sheet with foil and spray with non-stick coating.

Toss potatoes and remaining ingredients in a bowl to coat and mix.

Line in a single layer on baking sheet and bake for 30 minutes.

Toss the cooked potatoes in 1 Tablespoon of melted butter and transfer to serving bowl.

Sprinkle with 1 Tablespoon of fresh parsley.

GENERATION 3

James (1912-1985) and Marianne (1915-2017) Gaccetta

Mom and Dad on their Honeymoon 1937

Mom and Dad in the Kitchen 1978

BREADS

And

DESSERTS

—◆⬥◆—

This section contains bread recipes and dessert dishes that do not qualify as cakes, pies, or cookies. You can practically smell these delectable dishes just by reading the titles! Enjoy trying your hand at breads and desserts.

AUNT MELLA'S BANANA BREAD

Aunt Mella was my mother's youngest sister. You will read about her a lot in *One Caregiver's Journey* since my cousin and I shared responsibility for her care for many years. Mom got this recipe and began making it regularly with "dead" bananas as I have always referred to bananas with brown, speckled skin. This is one of the easiest recipes and one of the tastiest banana breads ever. It is a family favorite.

Preheat oven to 350^0

Preheat a toaster oven to 325^0

Spray a loaf pan with non-stick spray.

Feeling lazy? Line the loaf pan with foil, leaving several inches over the edge. When cooked, just lift the banana bread out of the pan and peel the foil away to allow it to cool. Your loaf pan will be clean.

1 cube soften butter

1 cup sugar

1 ¾ cups all-purpose flour

1 teaspoon baking soda

1 teaspoon salt

1 cup mashed bananas (about 2 medium size bananas)

2 eggs

½ cup chopped nuts (optional)

Measure flour and salt in a bowl and set aside.

Mash bananas with baking soda in a bowl and set aside.

In a mixing bowl, cream butter and sugar thoroughly, scrape the bowl with a spatula and add eggs and mix. Alternate adding dry ingredients and bananas. Do not over beat this mixture. Put in a loaf pan. Bake for 50 minutes.

Let stand for 10 minutes and then cool on a rack.

BANANA MUFFINS

Preheat oven 400⁰

2 ripe bananas peeled and mashed

1 egg

½ cup sugar

¼ cup milk

¼ cup vegetable oil

1 teaspoon vanilla

1 cup all-purpose flour

1 cup quick rolled oats

1 teaspoon baking powder

½ teaspoon baking soda

½ cup butterscotch or chocolate chips (optional)

This makes 12 cupcake-sized muffins or 6 large muffins. Either spray muffin pan with non-stick coating or line the pan with cupcake baking liners. Set aside.

In a mixing bowl mix banana, eggs, sugar, milk, oil, and vanilla. Scrape bowl with spatula and stir in dry ingredients and chips. Spoon filling into the pan or liners ¾ full.

Bake 15-20 minutes.

REFRIGERATED BANANA SPLIT DESSERT

This is a fun dessert. This recipe lists the ingredients in the order the dessert is put together.

Crust:

2 cups graham cracker crumbs

¼ cup sugar

1 cube melted butter

Mix graham cracker crumbs, sugar, and butter together and spread in a 9 x 13 pan. Set aside.

Filling:

2 8 oz. packages softened cream cheese

2 cups sugar

1 teaspoon vanilla

Cream together cream cheese, sugar and vanilla and spread over crust.

Topping:

Slice 3 medium (yellow, not speckled, or ripe) bananas over cream cheese mixture.

Spread 1 20 oz. can drained pineapple over bananas

Spread 1 medium container Cool Whip over fruit like frosting.

Chill 2-3 hours to set.

To serve, sprinkle with chopped nuts on top, drizzle with chocolate syrup.

Serves 10-20.

Eleanor Gaccetta

BRAN MUFFINS

This is a good choice for breakfast on a weekend when there is time to bake something hearty and healthy.

Preheat oven to 400⁰

1¼ cup all-purpose flour

3 teaspoons baking powder

½ teaspoon salt

½ cup sugar

2 ½ cups 40% Brank Flakes cereal

1 ¼ cup milk

1 egg

1/3 cup vegetable oil

Mix all ingredients together in a large mixing bowl. Spray a 12-muffin pan with non-stick spray or line with paper cups. Fill the muffin holes ¾ full.

Bake 25 minutes.

NOTE: You can add jams and jellies in the middle of the muffins by placing 1 teaspoon of jam into ½ filled muffin and then cover with batter to make it ¾ full. This makes a nice "surprise" when eating.

HOMEMADE BREADSTICKS

This recipe came from a friend's mother. Grace Accamasso and Mom swapped recipes for several years. Grace's family was from Northern Italy and my mother's family was from Sicily. Their cooking styles were different, but their results were equally delicious. This recipe is a labor of love; it takes time and patience. But the result is well worth it!

2 cups warm water

1 package rapid rising yeast

1 teaspoon sugar

4 cubes (1 pound) butter softened - do not melt and do not substitute anything for the butter

2 cups all-purpose flour

1 teaspoon salt

6-7 cups flour for stiff dough

In a large mixing bowl. dissolve yeast and 1 teaspoon sugar in 2 cups warm water. Add 2 cups flour and let stand for 1 hour.

On a floured board or baking mat (baking surface) dump yeast/flour mixture and add softened butter, and salt. Knead in enough flour to make a stiff dough. Cover and let stand for 1 hour.

On a floured surface roll into breadsticks. Take dough and roll slightly larger than a pencil, line on an ungreased cookie sheet. This will make a lot of breadsticks and numerous cookie sheets.

Bake until light brown: Check them at 15 minutes and then at 5 minute intervals afterwards.

CINNAMON ROLLS

This is a variation to the normal version of cinnamon rolls. Mom found this recipe in a magazine and it became her go-to for large family brunch gatherings. She liked the texture and difference in taste and because Mom made them, they were always devoured quickly!

Combine and set aside:

1 cube butter softened

1/3 cup sugar

2-3 Tablespoons cinnamon

Dough:

1 package Duncan Hines Yellow cake mix, or French Vanilla cake mix

5 cups flour

2 packages rapid rise yeast

2 cups warm water

Combine cake mix, flour and yeast in a large mixing bowl and blend together. Stir in warm water and make dough. Cover and let it rise in a warm place for 1 hour until doubled in volume.

Preheat oven to 400⁰

Divide dough in half. Roll out on a floured surface into a rectangle. Spread butter, sugar, and cinnamon liberally over dough. From long side roll into a log and cut into one-inch rolls. Place in prepared pans, cover with dishcloth, and let stand for 1 hour. Repeat with other half of dough.

Cook at 400⁰ for 20-25 minutes.

You can frost with a mixture of powder sugar, melted butter, a dash of cinnamon, and milk.

CREAM PUFFS

Mom was the cream puff queen. Relatives would specifically request that she make cream puffs for various family gatherings throughout the year. Today I frequently make them for family gatherings. This is one of my brother's favorite desserts. Profiteroles is the correct culinary name for cream puffs. Making a pate a choux (say shoe) pastry is simple. Follow the fool-proof directions and your cream puffs will also be a hit.

Preheat oven to 375°

1 cube of butter

1 cup water

1 ½ teaspoons sugar

½ teaspoon salt

1 cup of all-purpose flour

4 eggs

In a heavy saucepan bring butter, salt, sugar, and water to a rolling boil. Vigorously stir in the flour *with a wooden spoon* stirring until mixture leaves the side of the pan for forms a ball. Stir and cook for 1-2 minutes. Remove from heat and transfer the mixture to a mixing bowl with the paddle running. Beat in the eggs one at a time until the mixture is smooth and velvety.

Line a baking sheet with parchment paper and drop mixture by spoonful onto paper. Try to make 2-inch rounds. Leave sufficient room between for the puffs to rise while cooking.

NOTE: The larger the spoon, the larger the profiterole.

Bake 25-30 minutes until dry. May require longer baking time. Do not remove until cooked. Cool completely on a rack. When ready to fill, slice in the middle and fill with whipped cream or Cool Whip. For a surprise, drizzle chocolate syrup in bottom of one side before the adding cream.

BASIC CREPES

My cousin Dorothy Hecht gave Mom this recipe one Easter when she wanted to make something different for a Palm Sunday. This crepe can be filled with dessert toppings such as berries and sweetened cream cheese or as a manicotti crepe for a main dish.

Sift together in a bowl:

1 ½ cups all-purpose flour

1 teaspoon baking powder

½ teaspoon salt

1 Tablespoons sugar

In a mixing bowl beat:

2 eggs

2 cups milk

Add eggs and milk to dry ingredients and mix well until smooth.

Butter a non-stick skillet set to medium heat after each crepe. Pour small amount of batter in pan, swirl to coat the pan. Turn with a spatula and cook briefly on the other side. Remove to a plate and repeat.

Makes 11 good sized crepes.

GLORIFIED RICE SALAD

My mom started making this salad as a side dish for large winter gatherings, but it somehow began showing up at the table for summer gatherings as well. Many varieties of canned fruits can be used, but she always stuck to this basic salad. Today, my nieces still serve it as an additional dish at family gatherings. It is always a hit.

3 cups long grain rice–cooked, drained, and rinsed until shiny

¾ cup sugar

1 large can fruit cocktail

1 large can crushed pineapple drained

In a large bowl mix rice, sugar, and fruit. Chill overnight.

Next morning add:

1 pint whipping cream or large carton of Cool Whip

1 package miniature marshmallows

1 cup toasted coconut

Top with vanilla wafer crumbs and maraschino cherries.

Serves a crowd!

GREBBLES

This is a German donut recipe and will yield approximately 4 dozen. My mother grew up in a neighborhood with a German family, The Millers. A mother and daughter (Bertha and Esther) married two brothers (Gus and Otto.) The daughter, Esther, ran a local bar. After going to market, farmers and truckers would stop there on the way home for a cup of coffee. Esther made these donuts daily and shared the recipe with my mom.

12 oz. sour cream

3 eggs

1 cup sugar

1 teaspoon baking soda

teaspoon baking powder

1teaspoon salt

4 cups all-purpose flour

1 Tablespoon vanilla

½ teaspoon cinnamon

½ teaspoon nutmeg

Vegetable oil for frying

Sift flour, baking soda, baking powder, salt, cinnamon, and nutmeg, and set aside.

In a large mixing bowl: Beat eggs and sugar until creamy, gradually adding sour cream and vanilla. Add dry ingredients into the creamed mixture and mix into a soft dough.

Take half the dough and place on a floured surface. Roll to ¼ inch thickness. And cut into squares. Repeat until all the dough is used.

Heat oil to 375⁰ and fry donuts until brown, turning once. Remove from oil and drain on paper towels.

These can be rolled in powdered sugar, granulated sugar, cinnamon sugar, or eaten plain.

ICE BOX DESSERT

This was an occasional dessert Mom would make to bring to a relative's house or when there was a large gathering. I might add, when we were growing up, all gatherings were large. This dessert is from her American recipe collection.

1 box crushed vanilla wafers

3 cups powdered sugar

4 eggs

1 cup (2 cubes) softened butter

1 large can crushed pineapple drained

1 cup chopped walnuts

2 bananas

1-pint heavy whipping cream

Whip cream with 1 Tablespoon sugar or use 1 large container Cool Whip.

Spread ½ vanilla wafers on bottom of a 9 x 13 pan and set aside.

In a mixing bowl: Beat eggs, add powdered sugar and butter until smooth. Spread over vanilla wafers. Add drained pineapple and spread cream or whipped topping over pineapple. Add nuts and bananas. Top with remaining ½ of vanilla wafers.

Chill for 24 hours.

ITALIAN RICOTTA CHEESE PIE

This pie is an Easter tradition for many Italian families. Growing up Mom would make several pies to serve for either Palm Sunday or Easter Sunday dinner. The pie has a custard-like texture and this recipe is for two variations: a sweet pie and a savory pie. Either way, one thing is for certain - the aroma in the house will tickle your senses.

Preheat oven to 350^0

Crust: In a mixer with a dough hook combine:

1 cube softened butter

½ cup Crisco butter

2 eggs

½ cup sugar

3 cups all-purpose flour

1 teaspoon baking powder

2-3 Tablespoons milk

Mix dough until a ball forms. Roll on a floured surface to ¼ inch thickness. Place into your baking pan and set aside. This makes enough for 2-9 x 9 pans or 1-9 x 13 pan.

Pie #1 Sweet Pie

2 lbs. ricotta cheese, drained

½ cup corn starch

6 eggs

2 teaspoons vanilla or orange extract

In a large mixing bowl, add all the ingredients and whip together. Pour into a prepared crust. Set baking dish on a cookie sheet and bake for 1 hour or until the center is set.

Pie #2 Savory Pie (Sausage)

1 ½ lbs. ricotta cheese drained

1 lb. bulk sausage, cooked, drained, and chopped

½ cup corn starch

6 eggs

3 Tablespoons Romano cheese

In a large mixing bowl, add all the ingredients and whip together. Pour into a prepared crust. Set baking dish on a cookie sheet and bake for 1 hour or until center is set.

To serve either pie use a sharp knife to cut through crust and make small slices. These are very rich so slices should be small.

Eleanor Gaccetta

PEACHY MARMALADE

This is a canning recipe. Before store bought jams and jellies were readily available year-around, women would preserve seasonal fruits such as peaches, plums, and pears through a canning process. Mom made this thick marmalade in the fall and stored it in jars for winter enjoyment.

18 peaches, scalded and skinned

5 oranges quartered with rind

1 cup maraschino cherries chopped

1 cup sugar for every cup puree

In a large bowl, cut peaches into quarters and set aside. In a food processor puree peaches. Measure liquid volume and put in a large saucepan. Chop quartered oranges in a food processer–*do not chop too fine.* Add to peaches. Add 1 cup sugar for every cup of puree.

Cook mixture to a rolling boil stirring often to prevent sticking. When liquid covers (sheets) spoon, add the cherries and continue stirring. Reduce heat and cook for another 10 minutes.

Set aside to cool. Place in jars and seal with paraffin wax prior to putting on lids. Store in a cool place.

POTICIA

Poticia is a European dessert. This recipe is time consuming and difficult. This is not for the weekend warrior looking for something to do or the novice baker. Mom would make this recipe occasionally for Christmas holidays, if she had an extra day. This makes a large portion and she would often share with friends and relatives as a gift.

Bread:

2 ½ cups all-purpose flour

1 package yeast

1/3 cup milk

¼ cup (1/2 cube) softened butter

2 Tablespoons sugar

½ teaspoon salt

2 eggs

In a medium bowl combine 1 cup flour and yeast and set aside. In a saucepan heat milk, sugar, butter, and salt. Add to flour and yeast. Add eggs and mix with dough hook. Add remaining flour with a wood spoon and mix until a ball forms.

Knead on floured surface until dough is soft, smooth, and elastic. Set aside, cover and let rise for 1-1/2 hours.

Filling:

3 cups ground walnuts

¾ cup sugar

¼ cup melted butter

1 egg slightly beaten

3 Tablespoons milk

½ teaspoon vanilla

1 teaspoon grated lemon or orange zest

¼ cup honey

In a mixing bowl stir together all the ingredients and set aside.

To assemble:

Cut dough in half. And roll one portion on a floured surface to measure a 30 x 10 sheet. Roll carefully and evenly.

Spread half the filling over the sheet within one inch of edges. From short edge roll tightly and evenly. Pinch ends to seal. Place roll seam side down on a parchment lined cookie sheet. Repeat with other half of dough. Cover and let rise for 45-60 minutes.

Preheat oven to 325^0

Bake for 45-50 minutes. Cool before slicing.

PEANUT BUTTER PIE

Preheat oven to 450⁰. Then reduce to 350⁰.

Set aside a pre-made pie shell.

Cream together:

1 cup peanut butter

1 teaspoon vanilla

Add:

1 ½ cups sugar

½ teaspoon salt

2 eggs

1 ½ cups milk

Pour mixture into the pie shell.

Bake at 450⁰ for 10 minutes. Reduce heat to 350⁰ and bake for 20-25 minutes until knife inserted into the middle comes out clean.

Eleanor Gaccetta

SWEET EASTER BREAD

This recipe has been in the family for generations and is an Italian Easter tradition. Originally it called for spoons of lard, salt in the palm of your hand and, bottles of milk. My mom's sister-in-law (my Aunt Louise Spano) measured all the ingredients diligently one Easter season so that the bread would turn out consistently every time. In addition to Easter, Aunt Louise would sell this bread at the Georgetown Christmas Market, a small mountain community where her daughter, Rosemary Laurita, and family lived and had a restaurant for many years. My mother would double this recipe to ensure everyone got a loaf of bread with a piece of palm from Palm Sunday as a symbol of good luck. I am one of the few remaining relatives who makes this for Easter. It is a time consuming labor of love. But nothing can compare to enjoying a slice of hot bread, fresh from the oven, and slathered with butter after a long day in the kitchen.

This recipe makes 8 one-pound loaves of bread. It can be halved.

6-7 pounds of bread flour

2 cups warm water

2 teaspoons sugar

5 packages rapid rise yeast

1 quart warm milk (can be 2 cans of evaporated milk and water to make a quart, or regular milk)

2 cubes butter

12 eggs beaten (always use extra-large eggs or add more if using smaller eggs)

2 cups sugar

3 Tablespoons salt

½ lb. Crisco butter

In a *large* pan (I use a metal dishpan or extra-large stainless-steel bowl) warm milk and melt butter on low heat. Do not make mixture too hot for your touch. Remove from heat. In a 2-cup measure cup mix yeast, 2 teaspoons sugar, and 2 cups warm water. Set aside allow to bloom.

Using your hands, incorporate eggs, sugar, and salt into milk and butter. Add yeast and slowly incorporate flour. Once the dough comes together coat sides and bottom of pan with Crisco butter. Continue adding four to make a soft dough. Cover and let rise in a warm place for 1 hour. Punch dough down and let it rise a second time.

Preheat oven to 325⁰

On a greased baking mat (use Crisco butter) measure and weigh one-pound increments of dough. Knead to form a loaf. Generously grease loaf pans and add bread. Cover and let raise for 30-45 minutes.

Bake at 325⁰ for 20-25 minutes. If oven has a convection setting use it. Many ovens will allow for 3-5 pans to be baked at the same time–leave space between pans and sides of the oven. Bread may not brown evenly so it may be necessary to shift pans during baking.

After removing from the oven, turn loaves out of the pan on wire racks to cool and brush with Crisco butter while warm.

SWEET MUFFINS

This is a great quick breakfast bread. I would bake these often on Saturday mornings for Mom. They can be filled with jam or jelly for an extra surprise. They are filling and great when served with a slice or two of bacon.

Preheat oven to 400⁰

1 egg

½ cup milk

¼ cup vegetable oil

1 ½ cups all-purpose flour

½ cup sugar

2 teaspoons baking powder

½ teaspoon salt

1/2 teaspoon jam or jelly (optional)

In a medium size bowl combine flour, sugar, baking powder, and salt together and set aside

In a small bowl or mixing cup combine egg, milk, and vegetable oil. Add to the dry ingredients and mix until well incorporated.

Line muffin tin with papers or spray with non-stick spray. Fill the cups ¾ full. Fill cups ½ full if you wish to add jam or jelly and then fill with remaining dough.

Bake 15-20 minutes.

SWEET CHEESE MUFFINS

This is a variation of the sweet muffin that is served by a local donut shop. This is a sweet, tangy variation of the regular sweet muffin.

Preheat oven to 400⁰

1 egg

½ cup milk

¼ cup vegetable oil

1 ½ cups all-purpose flour

½ cup sugar

2 teaspoons baking powder

½ teaspoon salt

½ teaspoon baking soda

1/3 brick softened Neufchatel cheese

In a small bowl mix flour, sugar, baking powder, salt, and baking soda and set aside.

In a medium bowl beat egg, milk, oil, sugar, and cheese until smooth. Add dry ingredients and mix well.

Line 6 or 12 count muffin tin with non-stick spray. Fill each muffin cup ¾ full.

Bake 15 minutes for 6 large muffins.

Bake 20 minutes for 12 regular muffins.

Eleanor Gaccetta

FRUIT PIE

In addition to being a great cook, my mother was a masterful baker. When peaches, berries, apples, or other fresh fruit was in season (late summer and fall) the house would smell like a variety of fresh baked fruits. My dad loved apple pie and Mom's pie would be loaded over the top with spicy cooked apples. Mom would cook and freeze bags of apples so she could make dumplings or pies all winter. My dad would help peel large boxes of apples that he would buy at the local market. She also made a prized lemon meringue pie!

Rule of thumb:

Any fresh fruit recipe can be substituted with two large cans of pie filling.

Lemon pies are best when made with Cook and Serve lemon filling (2 large boxes).

Generally, it will take 4 or more cups of fresh fruit to make a full-bodied pie.

Apple pies will generally require 6 large apples (any baking variety) can be cooked or raw.

Peach pie will generally require 6-8 large peaches, peeled, and sliced, generally raw.

Cherry or berries should be a mixture of cooked (with sugar) and raw fruit.

NOTE:

For fresh fruit pies, slice and place in a bowl and add:

½ cup sugar

Liberally add: 1 teaspoon each cinnamon, nutmeg, and allspice.

Mix and pour into pie crust. Make a slurry with ¼ cup cornstarch and water and pour over fruit. (a slurry will thicken the juices as the pie cooks.) Add top crust and bake.

Baking:

Preheat oven to 400⁰

Always put pies on a cookie sheet to catch any juice that might escape or boil over the top.

Bake for 1 ½ hours. Cool completely before slicing.

NOTE: Pies are best when baked in a glass pie dish.

Pie dough recipes are on pages 102 and 103.

MERINGUE FOR PIES

Oven to 350⁰

Combine 1/3 cup sugar and 1 Tablespoon cornstarch in a small bowl and set aside.

In a large bowl combine:

5 egg whites

½ teaspoon cream of tartar

2 Tablespoons marshmallow cream (optional)

Whip until soft peaks form. Add the sugar mixture, 1 Tablespoon at a time beating until stiff peaks form. You can add marshmallow cream and incorporate.

Spoon meringue over pie (lemon or chocolate) and bake until the peaks are light brown (about 12 minutes). Keep an eye on the oven so the peaks do not burn.

SANDY'S PIE CRUST

Sandy Stabile is a good family friend who is known for her pies and particularly her pie crust. There are many different variations of pie crusts, and I think we have tried them all. Mom rated this one a 5-star ***** crust.

Double this recipe if your pie calls for both a top and bottom crust.

1 ½ cups all-purpose flour

½ teaspoon salt

¾ cup shortening (soft)

1 egg beaten

½ Tablespoon white vinegar

2-3 Tablespoons cold water

Sift flour and salt in a bowl. Add shortening and cut into flour mixture with two knives. Add egg, vinegar, and water. Mix but do not handle too much as heat from your hands will affect the texture. Roll into a ball, wrap in plastic wrap, and refrigerate for 30 minutes.

If making a double recipe for top and bottom crusts, cut ball in half.

Roll dough between two sheets of wax paper. Remove top sheet and gently turn the dough into the clean, dry pie dish.

This crust can be pre-baked at 425° for 25 minutes. Cool for custard or cream fillings.

Eleanor Gaccetta

SUPER PIE CRUST

This was a general, easy go-to crust for Mom. She would sometimes just make the pie crust, roll it out, and cut into silly shapes and put them in a cookie tin. She would sprinkle with sugar and cinnamon and bake at 425^0 for 15 minutes for an after-school treat during the winter. Pie crust doesn't always have to be for a pie!

For 2 crusts:

3 cups flour

6 Tablespoons powdered sugar

6 Tablespoons butter-chilled

4 ½ Tablespoons lard or shortening-chilled

¼ cup or less ice water

Place flour, sugar, butter and lard in a food processer and blend until coarse. Add 4 Tablespoons water, blend and continue adding water until dough forms into a soft ball.

NOTE: Most pie crust recipes require refrigeration for at least 30 minutes to ensure a flaky pie crust. This recipe did not require refrigeration. I would recommend refrigerating for 30 minutes to chill before rolling it out.

Cut dough in half and set half aside. Transfer ball to a floured baking surface. Roll out between two sheets of wax paper. May need additional flour for rolling. Remove top sheet and gently place the pie dough into a pie pan.

CAKES

—◆✦◆—

My mother loved to bake cakes. This section includes some of the most delicious cake recipes you will find. I have shared her secrets for making homemade frosting and homemade vanilla extract. Bake a cake and watch your loved ones smile!

GENERATION 4

Eldest Brother - Sam (1939-2001) and Jackie

"Other Brother" Don and Connie (1946-2020)

Eleanor Gaccetta

Me - Eleanor Gaccetta

MAKE YOUR OWN VANILLA EXTRACT

My mother always used only pure vanilla extract for baking. Mom believed in using only the finest ingredients for baking, never substitutes. Her mantra was, "If you're going to put in the time, energy, and effort to bake, you need to use butter, the largest eggs you can find and pure extracts." Mom was adamant that whether you were baking for yourself, for company, or for a gift, you always used highest quality ingredients. Today the cost of pure vanilla from the food specialty stores is more than $50 a bottle. Several years ago, I did some research and decided to start making my own vanilla. It is an easy process but using quality ingredients is not inexpensive. You will never buy another bottle of vanilla.

NOTE: Buy a brand of vodka you would enjoy drinking. Do not buy cheap vodka, the vanilla beans will not ferment, and your baked goods will taste like cheap alcohol.

1 quart Vodka

6-8 Vanilla beans

Split the vanilla beans lengthwise with a sharp knife to expose the pods.

Place the split vanilla beans into the bottle of vodka. Place in a dark place for up to six weeks before using. (I store mine in a cupboard in the basement.) Shake the bottle to mix the beans every few days for the first few weeks. Transfer as needed to a dark glass bottle for use in baking.

HOMEMADE FROSTING

Today it is far easier to just grab a can of frosting from the grocery shelf in the baking aisle. My mother made this basic recipe for all her cakes. Flavorings are added as necessary, lemon, orange, chocolate, vanilla, etc. Growing up my mom made two chocolate cakes each week during the winter, one for Sunday company and one for my dad and brother to take in their lunches during the week.

Basic Butter Frosting

1 ½ cubes softened butter

3 cups powdered sugar

3 Tablespoons milk

1 teaspoon vanilla

Melt the butter, add milk and vanilla, and incorporate powdered sugar. Stir until frosting is a smooth consistency for spreading.

This recipe will frost 2-9 inch layers or 1- 9x13 pan.

Basic Chocolate Frosting

1 ½ cubes softened butter

1/3 cup cocoa powder

3 cups powdered sugar

3 Tablespoons milk

1 teaspoon vanilla

1 Tablespoon cooled coffee (optional if you like mocha taste)

Melt the butter, add milk, vanilla, and cocoa. Incorporate powdered sugar stirring until frosting is a smooth consistency for spreading.

This recipe will frost 2-9 inch layers or 1-9x13 pan.

To make flavored frostings, add 2 teaspoons zest and 2 teaspoons juice of a fresh lemon or orange to the basic butter recipe.

APPLE LOAF CAKE

Preheat oven to 350⁰

This is a variation of banana bread only with apples.

Topping:

Combine and set aside:

2/3 cup brown sugar

1 teaspoon cinnamon

Cake:

2/3 cup granulated sugar

1 cube softened butter

1 ½ teaspoon vanilla

2 eggs

½ cup milk

1 ½ cup all-purpose flour

1 ¾ teaspoons baking powder

1 apple peeled and chopped

Cream butter and sugar until smooth, add vanilla, milk, and eggs. Mix well scraping the bowl often. Add flour and baking powder, mix, and stir in apples.

Spray loaf pan with non-stick spray coating and put in ½ mixture. Top with half the

brown sugar and cinnamon. Add remaining batter and top with remaining cinnamon and sugar. Using a knife swirl the topping.

Bake 40 minutes.

Eleanor Gaccetta

APPLE UPSIDE DOWN CAKE

This is one of those delectable surprises! I decided to try something different for a Sunday afternoon visit from relatives while I was caring for Mom. I found this old newspaper recipe folded in one of Mom's cookbooks. It is super simple to make. My brother happened to drop by to visit just as I was struggling to invert the cast iron pan onto a serving dish. When he saw the caramel running down the sides of the dish and apples he was surprised. I think he ate about ¼ of the cake waiting for it to cool down! Since that time, it has been a family favorite.

Preheat oven to 375⁰

This cake is best if made in a mid-size cast iron pan. Can be made in a 9x13 pan but must be inverted onto a rectangle serving tray.

1 box Vanilla flavored cake mix

½ cup brown sugar, packed

3 Tablespoons butter melted

2 large apples, peeled, cored, and sliced

Arrange apples in bottom of pan in any design. Pour melted butter over apples and sprinkle brown sugar on top.

Bake cake according to instructions on the box and pour over apples.

Bake 35-40 minutes.

Let sit 5 minutes and invert onto a serving dish and allow to cool.

In my home this cake is generally eaten while it is warm.

BETTER THAN SEX CAKE

I got this cake from a co-worker and Mom always thought it was a good recipe, but she was not very fond of the name. I baked it often just to see her react!

Preheat oven to 350⁰

1 package Duncan Hines yellow cake mix

1 small package instant vanilla pudding

1 package German chocolate baking bar grated

8 oz. sour cream

3 eggs

½ cup vegetable oil

6 oz. chocolate chips

½ cup chopped nuts (walnuts or pecans)

1 ½ cup water

In a large bowl mix cake mix, pudding, sour cream, eggs oil and water. Mix well scraping the bowl often. Fold in nuts and chocolate chips and ½ grated chocolate. Pour into a 9x13 pan sprayed with non-stick spray. Bake for 45 minutes. Cool and Frost.

Frosting:

1 cube softened butter

2 cups (or more) powdered sugar

½ cup chopped nuts

3 oz. cream cheese softened

1 teaspoon vanilla

Mix butter and cream cheese, add vanilla, and incorporate powdered sugar. When frosting is a smooth consistency stir in nuts.

Spread on a cooled cake and sprinkle with remaining grated chocolate.

CARROT CAKE

This is a family favorite and Mom would often bring this to a family gathering at someone's house. This recipe feeds a crowd and requires patience to gather all the ingredients.

Preheat oven to 350⁰

In a large baking bowl add:

2 cups all-purpose flour
2 cups sugar
1 cup vegetable oil
2 cups finely shredded carrots
1 cup angle flaked coconut
1 cup crushed pineapple, drained
1 ½ teaspoons baking soda
2 teaspoons cinnamon
2 teaspoons vanilla
2 cups chopped nuts
1 teaspoon salt
3 eggs

Mix well and pour into a greased 9x13 pan. Bake 40 minutes until a toothpick in the middle comes out dry. Cool.

Cream Cheese Frosting:

1 package softened cream cheese

½ cube melted butter

2-3 Tablespoons milk

½ teaspoon vanilla

2 cups powdered sugar—might need more

Mix cream cheese and butter until combined. Add milk, vanilla, and powdered sugar.

Frost top of the cake.

SEMI-HOMEMADE CARROT CAKE

Preheat oven to 350⁰

1 box Carrot Cake mix

1 box instant Vanilla pudding mix

½ cup water

½ cup vegetable oil

4 eggs

1 8 oz can crushed pineapple drained

½ cup nuts

½ cup shredded carrots

½ cup coconut

In a mixing bowl, combine cake mix, pudding, water, oil, and eggs. Scrape the bowl and add pineapple, carrots, nuts, and coconut. Mix until blended.

Spray a 9x13 pan with non-stick spray. Pour batter into the pan and bake according to the cake mix recipe.

Frost with cream cheese frosting from page 111.

CHEESECAKE

This recipe was introduced to our family by my sister-in-law, Jackie. It quickly became a family favorite for holidays and my mother loved to bake it as well. Today you can buy cheesecake in a variety of flavors, but there is nothing like a showstopper homemade cheesecake.

Preheat oven to 350°

Crust:

1 cup graham cracker crumbs

½ cup finely chopped walnuts

½ cup (1 cube) melted butter

Sugar to taste

Mix all the ingredients in a small bowl. Press the crumbs on the bottom and 1 inch up the sides of a *spring form* pan. Set aside.

Filling:

3 packages of cream cheese softened

1-12 oz. container sour cream

6 eggs

1 Tablespoon lemon juice

2 Tablespoons cornstarch

2 teaspoons vanilla

1 ½ cups sugar

In a large mixing bowl beat cream cheese, eggs, and sour cream until smooth. Add sugar, cornstarch, lemon, and vanilla. Beat until smooth. Pour into crust.

Bake 1 hour, turn off oven and leave in oven for 1 additional hour. **DO NOT** open oven door.

This can be topped with cherry pie filling or drizzled with caramel sauce when serving.

CHOCOLATE ALMOND CHEESECAKE

This is a "fancy" cheesecake that Mom would serve when special company was coming. The presentation is one that will wow any crowd, large or small.

Preheat oven to 350⁰

Crust:

1 8 oz. package chocolate cookies finely crushed
½ cup (1 cube) butter melted

Combine butter and crumbs and press firmly in bottom and up 2 inches on the side of a 9 inch *spring form* pan and chill.

Filling:

3 8 oz. packages cream cheese softened
¾ cup sugar
4 eggs
1 small package chocolate pieces melted and cooled
2 cups sour cream
½ cup Amaretto liqueur
4 Tablespoons (1/2 cube) butter
1 teaspoon vanilla

In a large bowl beat cream cheese and sugar until fluffy. Add eggs one at a time scraping bowl often. Blend in chocolate, one cup sour cream, ¼ cup Amaretto, 4 Tablespoons butter, and vanilla. Place chilled spring form pan on a cookie (baking) sheet and pour cheesecake batter over the crust. Bake 65 minutes.

Stir together remaining sour cream and Amaretto and spread over cheesecake. Return to oven for 3 minutes. Remove and cool. Cover and chill.

NOTE: The reason this is baked on a cookie sheet is that the butter tends to leak from the pan. Save yourself the brain damage of having to clean baked butter from the bottom of the oven.

CHIFFON CAKE

This is the five-star cake recipe of my mother's! She found this recipe in a Betty Crocker cookbook, 1961 vintage, and began making it for special occasions. She would make a mountain of marshmallow frosting and cover it with coconut. Mom gave the recipe to my Aunt Jennie and a competition started that lasted until their deaths over who could bake the highest, most air-filled cake. They both claimed the cake as their own and no one else in the family would bake it because it was just too much work. Today, three of us bake it while others still complain it is too much work. To be more health conscious, we no longer frost with a mountain of marshmallow frosting. Instead we us more of a light drizzle glaze. My cousin, Jerry, calls this the "State Fair" cake! This is a beautiful creation to make.

Preheat oven to 350⁰

This recipe requires a special chiffon cake pan – a large pan with a tube in the middle.

This recipe requires two bowls, one for egg whites and one for the cake mixture.

2 ¼ cups sifted *cake* flour

1 ½ cups sugar

3 teaspoons baking powder

1 teaspoon salt

Combine the above ingredients in a large bowl sift once and then sift again into your large mixing bowl. Sift *two* times. Make a well and add:

½ cup vegetable oil

¾ cups cold water

1 Tablespoon vanilla

2 teaspoons grated lemon or orange zest (optional)

6 egg yolks (use jumbo or extra-large eggs)

In a separate mixing bowl add:

½ teaspoon cream of tartar

1 ½ cups egg whites–whites from the 6 eggs above + whites from one or two additional eggs

Whip egg whites to stiff peaks on medium-high speed.

Mix cake ingredients with a large spatula until combined thoroughly and batter is smooth.

Add cake mixture to egg whites folding constantly until blended. Do not stir. Folding adds air and results in a light, fluffy, airy cake.

Pour into clean, dry chiffon pan.

Bake 50-55 minutes.

Cool upside down on a bottle that fits into the hole in the middle. Do not lay on a flat surface or on a cake rack.

When cool using a sharp knife slide the knife along the side of the pan and turn pan to cut evenly. Turn the pan over on serving dish and slide knife under bottom of pan and carefully slide the knife to cut.

This cake can be served naked or frosted with a simple drizzle or frosting.

CHOCOLATE CAKE FROM SCRATCH

My mother was known for her chocolate cakes. The problem is that Mom's recipe was in her head and never written on paper. My brother has asked me to try to find a recipe that comes close to Mom's. This is the closest we have found. He often eats chocolate cake for breakfast.

Preheat oven to 350⁰

Spray with non-stick baking spray or line with waxed paper–two 8x8, 9x9, or a 9x13 pan. Set aside.

2 cups sugar

1 ¾ cups all-purpose flour

¾ cup cocoa powder

1 ½ teaspoons baking powder

1 ½ teaspoons baking soda

1 teaspoon salt

2 eggs

1 cup milk

½ cup vegetable oil

2 teaspoons vanilla

1 cup boiling water

In a large bowl mix sugar, flour, cocoa, baking powder, baking soda, and salt. Mix thoroughly, make a well and add eggs, milk, vegetable oil, vanilla, and water. Mix 2 minutes, batter will be dark and thin. Pour into prepared pan(s). Bake round pans 30-35 minutes and 9x13 for 40-45 minutes. Cool before frosting.

Frosting:

1 cube softened butter

1/3 cup cocoa

1 teaspoon vanilla

3 Tablespoons milk

3 cups powdered sugar

Mix all ingredients together in a medium size bowl. You may need more powdered sugar to reach spreadable consistency. Spread on cake and enjoy.

Eleanor Gaccetta

CHOCOLATE CHERRY CAKE

Preheat oven to 350^0

1 box Chocolate cake mix

1 12 oz. can Cherry pie filling

3 eggs

1 teaspoon almond extract

In a bowl, mix cake, oil, and eggs with a spatula until smooth. **Fold** in cherries and almond flavoring. Do not stir.

Spray a 9x13 pan with non-stick spray. Pour batter and bake for 30 minutes. Cool and frost

Frosting:

1 cube butter softened

2-3 cups powder sugar

½ teaspoon almond (or vanilla)

1 teaspoon milk

In a bowl mix butter and 1 cup powdered sugar. Add milk and almond. Continue adding powdered sugar until mixture is a spreadable consistency. Frost your cake.

CINNAMON CHOCOLATE CHIP CAKE

Preheat oven to 350⁰

1 cube butter softened

1 ½ cup sugar divided

2 eggs

1 cup sour cream

1 teaspoon vanilla

2 cups all-purpose flour

1 ½ teaspoon baking powder

1 teaspoon baking soda

½ teaspoon cinnamon

1 12 oz bag chocolate chips

In a bowl combine flour, baking powder, and baking soda and set aside.

In a mixing bowl cream butter and 1 cup sugar, add eggs, sour cream, and vanilla. Scrape bowl often with spatula. Gradually add flour mixture and combine thoroughly.

Prepare 9x13 pan with non-stick cooking spray. Pour ½ batter into baking dish and add ½ package chocolates and ½ of the cinnamon and ½ remaining sugar. Pour remaining batter and sprinkle with remaining chips, cinnamon, and sugar.

Bake 30 minutes.

Eleanor Gaccetta

DIRT CAKE

This is a fun cake for a child's party. I got the recipe from a friend and gave it to family members who wanted to do something different for a child's birthday celebration. Spoiler Alert – this is a very unconventional way to write and explain a recipe.

1. Crush 2 20 oz. packages of Oreo cookies in a blender.

2. Mix two packages of French Vanilla pudding with 2 cups of milk and set aside.

3. Mix and set aside:

1 8 oz. package cream cheese softened

½ cup (1 cube) butter softened

3 Tablespoons powdered sugar

Combine #2 and #3 with a 12 oz. tub of Cool Whip.

In one large or 2 small plastic flowerpots layer cookies with the cheese/pudding mix starting and ending with the Oreo cookies (a/k/a dirt).

Decorate with flowers or gummy worms.

For more fun – serve with a potting trowel.

OLD FASHIONED DONUTS

This recipe was given to my mother by Ann Dailey, a long-time friend and nurse. Before Dunkin or grocery chain baked goods, women made donuts for their families. Growing up as a child, I remember my mother making donuts on a regular basis. She would roll out the dough and cut the rounds and holes with a special cutter. This is a labor of love. Quick to make and enjoy.

Vegetable oil for frying

3 cups all-purpose flour

1 cup sugar

¾ cup buttermilk

2 Tablespoons shortening (Crisco)

2 teaspoons baking powder

1 teaspoon salt

½ teaspoon nutmeg

In a large bowl add 1 ½ cups flour, sugar, buttermilk, shortening, baking powder salt and nutmeg. Mix on low speed constantly scraping the bowl. Increase speed to medium for 1 minute and return to low speed and add remaining flour. Scrape the bowl to incorporate the ingredients.

Refrigerate for at least one hour. Roll the dough on a well-floured pastry mat using a floured rolling pin to ½ inch thickness. Cut with a donut cutter. If you don't have a donut cutter, cut into squares or triangles. You can also just make a hole in the middle with your fingers to assure they will cook in the middle.

Heat vegetable or canola oil to 350⁰. Fry donuts and holes until brown turning to cook on both sides. Drain on paper towels.

You can frost or sprinkle warm donuts with sugar or powdered sugar.

DUMP CAKE

This recipe is just as the name suggests—you dump all the ingredients in the baking dish. My mother thought this was a fun recipe to make and she would make it occasionally for company. This cake will please pie lovers and cake lovers alike!

Preheat oven to 350^0

1 box yellow or French vanilla cake mix

1 can cherry pie filling

1 can crushed pineapple

1 cube butter – cut into small cubes or shaved

½ cup chopped pecans

Use a 9x13 pan

1. Dump cherry pie filling and spread evenly on bottom of dish.

2. Dump the cake mix evenly over the pie filling.

3. Dump the pineapple evenly over the cake mix.

4. Cover with pecans.

5. Place small cubes of butter (or shaved) over the pecans.

Bake at 350^0 according to the cake mix instructions.

PERFECT FUDGE BROWNIES

My late sister-in-law, Connie, was a brownie lover and my dad was a sweet lover. Mom would bake this recipe and eventually Connie started making it as well. This recipe makes 3 dozen brownies so it worked will for children and grandchildren for school celebrations. Serve with a cup of coffee or a glass of milk. This is a rich and decadent dessert.

Preheat oven to 375°

2 cubes butter

4 oz. unsweetened baking chocolate

1 ½ cups, plus 2 Tablespoons *sifted* flour

½ teaspoon baking powder

1 teaspoon salt

2 cups sugar

4 eggs slightly beaten

1 Tablespoon vanilla

¾ cup chopped nuts

Melt butter and chocolate over low heat and set aside.

Sift together flour, baking powder and salt.

In a large bowl, mix sugar and eggs until creamy. Add vanilla and cooled chocolate and butter, blending well. Add dry ingredients slowly and stir in nuts.

Pour batter into a greased 9 x 13 pan.

Bake 30-35 minutes–until a knife comes out clean.

Cool thoroughly.

Makes 3 dozen brownies.

FUDGE FROSTING

This recipe was originally used for the brownie recipe on the previous page, but it soon became a second chocolate frosting recipe that Mom loved to make. It is rich, decadent, and full of calories!

2 squares unsweetened chocolate

½ cube butter

5 Tablespoons milk

Pinch of salt

½ teaspoon vanilla

2 cups powdered sugar

Combine chocolate and butter in a double boiler on medium heat, stir until melted. Add salt and vanilla. Remove from heat and add powdered sugar. May need additional milk to stir to a spreadable consistency.

NOTE: If you do not have a double boiler pan. Put an inch of water in the bottom of a small saucepan and place a glass bowl on the pan. *Do not let the bowl touch the water.*

GERMAN CHOCOLATE CAKE

I remember the day my mother's cousin, Ginger Denton, taught us how to make this cake. The cake feeds 18-20 people. It is baked in large square pans or 3 round pans. This was Ginger's signature cake. However, family were quick to eat it but very shy about learning to bake because it is labor intensive. To make it right would consume an entire day. I have baked this cake once for an Easter dinner dessert of more than 30 people. This recipe underscores why baking is considered an art.

Preheat oven to 350^0

Generously grease 2–9 inch square pans or 3–8x8 inch round pans. Set aside.

½ cup boiling water

1 4 oz. bar Sweet cooking chocolate

2 cups sugar

1 cup (2 cubes) softened butter

4 egg yolks

2 teaspoons vanilla

1 ½ cups *cake* flour

1 teaspoon baking soda

1 teaspoon salt

1 cup buttermilk

4 egg whites stiffly beaten

Combine flour, baking soda, and salt and set aside.

Put chocolate in boiling water to melt.

In a large mixing bowl, cream butter and sugar. Scrape the bowl and add egg yolks and vanilla and mix well. Alternate adding dry ingredients and buttermilk and chocolate. *Fold* in the egg whites.

Pour into prepared pans and bake 35 minutes or until top springs back when touched or a toothpick comes out dry. Remove from pans and cool on wire racks.

Frost with Coconut Frosting on page 127.

COCONUT FROSTING

This is the frosting for the German Chocolate Cake frosting. However, it can be used for any cake.

1 cup sugar

1 cup evaporated milk

½ cup (1 cube) butter

3 egg yolks

1 teaspoon vanilla

1 1/3 cups flaked coconut

1 cup chopped pecans

Mix sugar, milk, butter, egg yolks, and vanilla in a 2-quart saucepan. Cook over medium heat for about 12 minutes. Stir in coconut and nuts. Stir until the mixture can be spread. Cool.

This is a naked cake. Place generous amount of frosting between the layers and on top of cake.

MILKY WAY CAKE

My mom found this recipe in the newspaper and decided it was a great way to use of left-over Halloween candy. The Bundt cake makes a nice presentation for guests or as a family alternative to a chocolate cake. This is an easy cake to make and Bundt cakes are easy to transport for special occasions.

Preheat oven to 350^0

In a saucepan on low to medium heat, melt 13 miniature Milky Way candy bars in ½ cup (1 cube) butter. Set aside.

Combine dry ingredients and set aside:

1 2/1 cups all-purpose flour

½ teaspoon baking powder

Combine wet ingredients and set aside:

1 ¼ cups buttermilk

1 teaspoon vanilla

In a large mixing bowl cream:

½ cup (1 cube) butter

2 cups sugar

4 eggs – add one at a time

Alternate adding dry ingredients with wet ingredients and mix well. Add melted candy bars. As an option you can stir in 1 cup chopped nuts.

Grease or liberally spray a Bundt pan. Pour batter into the pan.

Bake for 1 hour and 20 minutes.

Cool 10 minutes and remove from pan and finish cooling on a wire rack.

HOMEMADE PINEAPPLE UPSIDE DOWN CAKE

Before box cakes were sold and affordable, women baked desserts. My mother baked as much as she cooked primarily because my father had a sweet tooth. This cake is not difficult to make and it was always quickly devoured. I have baked the cake often mostly just to carry on a tradition of loving to spend time in the kitchen baking.

Preheat oven to 375^0

Fruit layer:

1 large can pineapple rings – drained

3 Tablespoons butter melted

½ cup brown sugar packed

Maraschino cherries

Arrange pineapple rings and cherries in the bottom of a glass pie plate or a 9-inch round cake pan. Pour melted butter over the pineapple and top with brown sugar. Set aside.

Cake:

2/3 cup brown sugar packed

½ cup butter softened

1 egg

1 teaspoon vanilla

1 ½ cups all-purpose flour

1 teaspoon baking powder

½ teaspoon salt

½ cup milk

Combine flour, baking powder, and salt in a bowl. Cream sugar and butter until fluffy. Scrape bowl add egg and vanilla and mix thoroughly. Alternate adding milk with flour mixture. Pour over pineapple mixture. Bake 35-40 minutes.

Remove from oven and invert into serving platter and let cool.

PUMPKIN CHEESECAKE

Preheat oven to 350⁰

Crust:

1 cup graham cracker crumbs

1 ½ cups crushed ginger snaps

5 Tablespoons melted butter

Mix crust and pat on bottom and up sides of a 9 ½ inch pie plate. Set aside.

Filling:

2-8 oz. packages cream cheese softened

1 cup sugar

1-16 oz. can pumpkin

2 teaspoons bourbon

1 teaspoon nutmeg

1 teaspoon cinnamon

In a mixing bowl cream, the cream cheese and sugar, scraping bowl often. Add pumpkin, bourbon, nutmeg, and cinnamon. Pour mixture into prepared pie plate.

Bake 40 minutes.

Cool before serving.

BUNNY CAKES FOR EASTER

Throughout many years of my childhood and well into my adult life, my mom made hundreds of bunny cakes for Easter. It was a tradition for all the grandkids, family, and special neighbor kids to receive a bunny cake. I vividly remember that there were years when we would make as many as 16 bunny cakes in a single day. Each would be decorated separately. Some would have white "fur" and others were colored from toasted coconut. This is one of my most cherished memories because it was a day we spent alone working from morning until night. Mom would put a card table in the living room, adorned with an Easter tablecloth, where the cakes would be displayed as they were finished. This was truly a labor of love and was greatly anticipated; all the kids loved receiving a Bunny Cake from Nana.

Preheat oven according to directions on box recipe.

1 box cake mix (your flavor choice) will make two bunny cakes.
1 recipe Marshmallow frosting (next page) will make them give them fluffy fur!

Bake the cake according to directions on the box for 2 8-inch round cakes. Cool completely.

To Assemble:

1. Cut a round layer into two half-moon shapes.

2. Stand the round so the half-moon shapes are together.

3. Cut a small wedge shape from one end about 1 ½ inches from bottom. Place the wedge at the opposite end of the cake. The wedge will become the tail and the opening will become the eyes, nose, and a place for the ears.

4. Place a liberal amount of frosting between the layers, adhere the tail with frosting and frost the remainder of the outside using a generous amount of frosting.

5. Cut ears from pink construction paper or white paper and color them pink with a crayon.

Use jellybeans for the eyes and nose (usually two pink and a black).

Admire your creation and then sit back, cut it, and enjoy!

MARSHMALLOW FROSTING

My mom's old cookbooks call this White Mountain Frosting. She made a mountain of it for sure through the years. This was her go-to frosting for special cakes. She preferred it over a buttercream and used it on Chiffon or birthday cakes most often. This is a very decadent frosting, rich and full of sugary calories. This frosting is wicked, crazy good. We stopped using it as we were making fewer bunny cakes for Easter and became more health conscious about indulging so much sugar in one sitting. The recipe can be cut in half for a normal two-layer cake.

This make enough frosting for 3 Bunny Cakes.

4 egg whites

3 cups sugar

½ teaspoon cream of tartar

2 Tablespoons light corn syrup

2/3 cup water

1 jar Marshmallow cream

In a large mixing bowl start to whip egg whites and cream of tartar on medium to medium-high speed.

Combine sugar, water, and corn syrup in a saucepan over medium heat. Once it comes to a boil stir constantly until mixture coats the back of the spoon.

Once egg whites are stiff slowly pour syrup mixture into egg whites. Be careful as the mixture will be HOT. Continue to whip on high and once the syrup is incorporated add marshmallow cream in small amounts incorporating well before adding more.

Frost your cake(s). Can decorate with coconut or colored sprinkles or shaved chocolate.

RHUBARB CAKE

My dad always had a couple of big rhubarb plants on the ditch bank of our farm. In the late spring, or early summer, the rhubarb would be ready to eat. Dad would generally cut and box the stalks and bring them to market to sell to restaurants. My Aunt Louise Spano found a recipe for this cake and the ladies decided to add this to their baking arsenal. It was baked one time a year when the plants were in season.

Preheat oven to 350°

2 cubes butter softened
1 ½ cups sugar
1 egg
1 cup buttermilk
2 cups all-purpose flour
1 teaspoon baking soda
1 teaspoon vanilla
½ teaspoon salt
3 cups rhubarb chopped in cubes

Mix flour, baking soda and salt in a bowl and set aside.

In a mixing bowl cream butter and sugar, scraping bowl often. Add egg, buttermilk, and vanilla, and add flour mixture mixing thoroughly and scraping bowl before folding in rhubarb.

Mix:

2 teaspoons cinnamon

½ cup brown sugar

1 Tablespoon softened butter

Sprinkle on top of batter.

Pour into a 9x13 pan sprayed with non-stick spray.

Bake 45-55 minutes.

BICARDI RUM CAKE

This was one of those cake recipes that was cut from a magazine and soon became one I would take to office potlucks. Mom would bake this cake occasionally and added it to her big box of recipes.

Preheat oven to 325^0

Liberally grease or spray a Bundt pan with non-stick cooking spray. Set aside

Cake:

1 package Yellow or French Vanilla cake mix
1 package Vanilla instant pudding mix
1 cup chopped pecans or walnuts
4 eggs
½ cup cold water
½ cup vegetable oil
½ cup dark rum

Sprinkle nuts on bottom of prepared pan.

Mix cake mix, pudding mix, eggs, cold water, vegetable oil and rum together, scraping the bowl.

Pour over the nuts in the pan.

Bake 1-hour.

Remove from the pan on a cake rack and cool.

Glaze:

1 cube butter
¼ cup water
1 cup sugar
½ cup dark rum

In a saucepan, melt butter, add water and sugar. Boil 5 minutes remove from heat and stir in rum.

Place the cake onto serving dish, prick top and side with holes. Drizzle glaze over holes until all is incorporated. Allow cake to absorb liquid.

ROYAL COCONUT CAKE

This is one of those interesting cakes with a very distinctive taste. My mom loved that the recipe since it calls for both vanilla and almond extracts. We would bake this cake occasionally when we had a taste for something out of the ordinary. I hope you enjoy it as much as we do if you try your hand at making it.

Preheat oven to 350^0

Cake:

3 cups all-purpose flour

1 teaspoon baking soda

1 teaspoon baking powder

½ teaspoon salt

1 ½ cubes butter softened

2 cups sugar

4 eggs

1 cup milk

1 Tablespoon vanilla extract

1 teaspoon almond extract

Mix flour, baking soda, baking powder, and salt in a bowl and set aside.

Cream butter and sugar. Scrape bowl and add eggs one at a time. Add milk, vanilla and almond and mix thoroughly. Slowly incorporate the flour mixture, scraping the bowl to mix thoroughly.

Spray 2-9-inch cake pans with nonstick cooking spray.

Bake 40-55 minutes.

Frosting:

1 large package cream cheese softened

1 cube butter softened

4-5 cups powdered sugar

½ teaspoon vanilla

1 teaspoon almond

2-3 Tablespoons milk

Mix to spreadable consistency. Frost cake and top with shredded coconut.

WALNUT GLORY CAKE

Preheat oven to 350°

9 eggs separated

1 ½ cups sugar divided in half

1 Tablespoon vanilla

¾ cup all-purpose flour

2 teaspoons cinnamon

1 teaspoon salt

2 cups walnuts finely chopped

Sift flour, cinnamon, and salt in a bowl and set aside.

In a mixing bowl, beat egg yolks until lightly colored and smooth. Gradually add ¾ cup sugar beating until the mixture is thick and lemon colored. Beat in vanilla. Add flour mixture to batter and beat until smooth. Set aside.

In another mixing bowl on high speed, whip egg whites into soft peaks adding remaining ¾ cup sugar one Tablespoon at a time. Fold ¼ of the whites into the cake batter and slowly add remaining egg whites. Fold in the walnuts.

Bake in a 10-inch tube pan sprayed with non-stick cooking spray.

Bake 45-55 minutes.

Cool and invert onto a serving dish.

ZEPPOLE (ITALIAN DONUTS)

This is a fun small treat that is generally served during the Christmas season. These little donuts are arranged on a tray like a Christmas tree, drizzled with honey and adorned with colored red and green sprinkles. Prying a piece off the Christmas tree is a gooey mess, but it is done with lots of smiles. My memory of this donut is from Christmas, but it could be enjoyed anytime.

Vegetable oil for frying

Mix ½ cup sugar and 2 Tablespoons cinnamon – set aside

3 Tablespoons sugar

1 cube butter

¼ teaspoon salt

1 cup water

1 cup all-purpose flour

4 eggs

In a saucepan melt butter, salt, sugar, and water. Bring to a boil. Remove from heat, stir in flour until blended. Return to heat and stir until mixture forms a ball. Transfer to mixing bowl and add eggs one at a time until incorporated and the mixture is smooth.

Heat vegetable oil to 350^0.

Drop batter in by the teaspoonful and fry. Roll in cinnamon sugar.

Makes 1-2 dozen.

COOKIES

This section is the cornerstone of my mother's baking arsenal. She loved to bake cookies of all varieties. Cookies are the grab-and-go food that gave the family a quick boost of energy in the middle of a day. Cookies were the comfort food that awaited us after school. Cookies just make you smile.

GENERATION 5 AND 6

Sam and Jackie's Family

Tom with my Mom

Tom's Son Jacob

Eleanor Gaccetta

Sam and Jackie's oldest daughter Cindy Generation 5

**Cindy's Children Nikalas, wife Haley and Shannon –
Generation 6**

Generation 5

Sam and Jackie's younger daughter Lisa with her husband John

Generation 6

Daughters Paige, Fallon and Haley

ALMOND LACE COOKIES

This is a delicate little cookie that tests skill and patience. It makes a beautiful addition to any platter of cookies to be served for a special occasion.

Preheat oven to 350⁰

¾ cup finely ground almonds

½ cup sugar

1 cube butter

1 Tablespoon all-purpose flour

2 Tablespoons milk

Grease a large cookie sheet.

Place all the ingredients in a 10-inch skillet. Cook over low heat stirring until butter is melted and ingredients are blended. Keep mixture warm over low heat.

Drop heaping teaspoonfuls of the mixture onto cookie sheet. Do not make more than 4 cookies at a time on the baking sheet.

Bake 5 minutes until golden.

Remove from pan with pancake spatula. Quickly loosen and turn cookies over one by one and roll around the handle of a wooden spoon to make a cylinder while warm. Cool on wire racks.

Repeat the process until all the batter is used. Grease cookie sheet between batches.

BASIC SHORTBREAD

There is little that is as good as a tasty shortbread cookie. You will find numerous recipes here that offer variations for the shortbread. My mother would occasionally make a shortbread cookie for us to enjoy. I bake them frequently.

Preheat oven to 350^0

3 cubes butter

1 cup powdered sugar

½ cup granulated sugar

1 Tablespoon vanilla

1 teaspoon salt

3 ½ cups all-purpose flour

Cream butter and sugars, scrape bowl with a spatula often and add vanilla and salt. Incorporate flour scraping bowl and mix until a soft ball forms.

Either make two flat disks or roll several small logs that are 2-inches in diameter. Refrigerate in plastic wrap for 2-3 hours. Disks can be rolled on a floured surface and cut into various shapes and sizes. Logs can be sliced into ¼ inch cookies.

Bake 20-25 minutes on a cookie sheet lined with parchment paper.

BAKLAVA PUFFS

My cousin, Elizabeth Talarico, shared this recipe with Mom and I many years ago. The traditional Jewish Baklava cookie was adjusted to be an easier recipe. In the days when many different variety Christmas cookies were made and displayed (and eaten), this was a favorite. I have not made these delectable little puffs of goodness in a while but may do so this year!

Preheat oven to 425⁰

1 cup walnuts or pecans finely chopped

1/3 cup honey

½ teaspoon cinnamon

1 package frozen puff pastry sheets

4 Tablespoons honey

Additional finely chopped nuts

Combine 1/3 cup honey, nuts and cinnamon and set aside.

Roll each pastry sheet into a 10-inch square on a floured surface. Cut into 2-inch squares. Place about ½ teaspoon of nut mixture in the center of each square. Moisten edges with water and fold at an angle to form a triangle. Press the edges to seal. Place on a cookie sheet lined with parchment paper and bake 13-15 minutes.

Heat 4 Tablespoons honey and brush tops and sprinkle with remaining nuts.

Makes 50 puffs.

BERRY SHORTBREAD DREAMS

Preheat oven to 350^0

1 cup butter softened

2/3 cup sugar

½ teaspoon almond extract

2 cups all-purpose flour

½ cup raspberry jam

In a bowl cream butter and sugar, scraping the bowl. Beat in the almond and gradually add flour until a soft dough forms.

Refrigerate in plastic wrap for 1 hour.

Make 1-inch balls. Line cookie sheet with parchment paper and place the balls one inch apart. Make an indentation in the top with your finger or the handle of a wooden spoon. Place ½ teaspoon raspberry jam into the hole.

Bake 14-18 minutes until the bottom is slightly brown.

BISCOTTI (ALMOND BARS)

This is not the classic biscotti recipe that is hard to eat because it is baked twice. My mother baked biscotti at least once a week for years. This is the quintessential cookie for dunking during afternoon (3:00 p.m.) coffee. Most biscotti are twice baked; this recipe is broiled. The result is a cookie that is easy to chew and flaky. The recipe makes several dozen cookies and they can be frozen or stored in an air-tight container. This is not a summertime cookie because butter is fickle and not a baker's friend when it is hot.

Preheat oven to 375^0

4 cubes (1 pound) butter softened
1 ½ cups sugar
4 eggs
4 cups all-purpose flour
1 teaspoon baking powder
1 Tablespoon Almond extract
2 cups *sliced* almonds

Cream butter, sugar, and eggs until smooth. Add almond flavor and part of the flour mixing well. Add remaining flour and baking powder and mix until you have a soft dough. Add almonds and mix well. On a floured surface roll dough into several 3-inch wide logs. Place logs on a parchment-lined cookie sheet. Most large cookie sheets will hold two logs.

Bake 20 minutes until the edges are browned remove from the oven and repeat until all the logs are baked. With a sharp knife slice logs into diagonal pieces, place cookies on their side and *BROIL* until tops are browned. Flip cookies and broil the other side.

NOTE: Do not leave the cookies unattended when broiling as this process occurs very quickly. The cookies are very hot when taking them from the broiler. Be careful turning to the opposite side so you don't end up with burned fingers. Rule of thumb is to alternate trays of cookies between broiling. Store in airtight container or can be frozen for up to a month in an airtight container.

Eleanor Gaccetta

CAKE COOKIES

Preheat oven to temperature on the box mix.

1 box chocolate cake mix (can use Yellow, White or French Vanilla)

½ cup (1 cube) butter softened

1 egg

1 cup walnuts

½ cup chocolate chips

½ cup cooled coffee

¼ cup all-purpose flour

1 teaspoon vanilla

In a large mixing bowl combine cake mix, butter, egg, coffee, flour, and vanilla. Mix thoroughly scraping the bowl often. Add nuts and chocolate chips and mix.

Drop onto a parchment lined cookie sheet.

Bake 12-14 minutes.

Cool on wire rack.

CHOCOLATE CHIP COOKIES

There are numerous different chocolate chip cookie recipes in this book. Mom had an arsenal of them because each has a slight variation and the result is a different texture and taste. Mom loved to diversify her baking recipes!

Preheat oven to 350⁰

½ cup (1 cube) butter

½ cup brown sugar packed

½ cup granulated sugar

1 egg

2 teaspoons vanilla

1 ½ cups all-purpose flour

2 teaspoons cornstarch

1 teaspoon baking soda

½ teaspoon salt

1 cup chocolate chips

Mix flour, cornstarch, baking soda, and salt in a bowl and set aside.

Cream butter and sugars until incorporated, add egg and vanilla and slowly incorporate the flour mixture.

Drop cookies by a rounded spoonful onto a parchment lined cookie sheet leaving 1 ½ inch space between them.

Bake 10-12 minutes.

Eleanor Gaccetta

HOME RUN CHOCOLATE CHIP COOKIES

This recipe is almost fool proof. It makes a large batch of cookies with a different texture due to the addition of vanilla pudding. This is a perfect cookie to send with children for school parties.

Preheat oven to 375^0

2 ¼ cups all-purpose flour

1 teaspoon baking soda

1 cup (2 cubes) butter softened

¼ cup granulated sugar

¾ cup light brown sugar firmly packed

1 teaspoon vanilla

1 package instant vanilla pudding

2 eggs

1 package chocolate chips

1 cup nuts chopped (optional)

Mix flour and baking soda in a bowl and set aside.

In a mixing bowl cream butter and sugars and add pudding mix. Mix until smooth scraping bowl with spatula. Add eggs and gradually add flour mixture. Stir in chips and nuts.

Drop dough by rounded teaspoons onto cookie sheet lined with parchment paper leaving 1 ½ inch space between.

Bake 10-12 minutes.

NOTE: This recipe can be cut in half.

CHOCOLATE RICOTTA COOKIES

There are three different cookies in this book made with Ricotta cheese, each with a very distinctive taste. These cookies became a favorite when helping my cousin, Paula Benallo, bake them for her oldest son's wedding. These are easy to make and attractive on a serving platter. Generally, they are baked "naked" or "lemon," but I learned that in Southern Colorado the Italian community makes them in chocolate. I baked them for a friend's granddaughter's wedding and what a hit! (This could be a soft chocolate chip cookie if you added chips.)

Preheat oven to 375°

2 cubes butter softened
2 cups sugar
1 15 oz. container Ricotta cheese
2 teaspoons vanilla
2 eggs
¼ cup cocoa powder
3 ¾ cups all-purpose flour
2 Tablespoons baking powder

Combine cocoa powder, flour and baking powder in a bowl and set aside.

Cream butter and sugar until mixed, add cheese, vanilla and eggs and mix thoroughly. Slowly incorporate the cocoa/flour mixture and mix until a soft dough. Scrape the bowl often.

Using a small ice cream scoop drop onto parchment lined cookie sheet. Leave about 1 inch between cookies.

Bake 12-15 minutes.

This cookie is best if removed from the oven when it looks slightly under-done. The texture will be moist and "pillowy."

Can be frosted with chocolate frosting or dusted with powdered sugar.

CINNAMON-SUGAR SPIRALS

This simple after-school treat can be made quickly when the kids arrive home from school and want something to eat after a long day.

Preheat oven to 350⁰

1 package refrigerated unbaked pie crusts

2 Tablespoons butter melted

In a bowl mix:

¼ cup sugar

1 ½ teaspoons cinnamon

Unroll pie crusts and brush lightly with butter. Sprinkle cinnamon sugar over crust. Roll pastry into a log, pinch and seal edge and ends.

Cut logs into ¼ inch slices. Place on a cookie sheet lined with parchment paper.

Bake 18-20 minutes.

COCONUT MACAROONS

Coconut was one of my mom's favorite additions for cookies or cakes. This recipe is a sweet, light variation of the traditional coconut cookie.

Preheat oven to 325⁰

2/3 cup all-purpose flour

5 ½ cups flaked coconut

½ teaspoon salt

1 can Eagle Brand Condensed milk

2 teaspoons vanilla

2 large egg whites

In a bowl mix with a wooden spoon the flour, coconut, salt, condensed milk, and vanilla until combined. Set aside.

Whip egg whites until soft peaks form and folk into the coconut mixture. Combine thoroughly.

Crop by heaping teaspoonful onto a cookie sheet lined with parchment paper.

Bake 23-25 minutes until coconut is toasted.

COCONUT MACAROONS

My mother always felt a lady should have options, so here is a second option for coconut macaroons! This one is more suited for holiday tray than a cookie jar.

Preheat oven to 325⁰

2 2/3 cups flaked coconut

2/3 cup sugar

¼ cup flour

¼ teaspoon salt

4 egg whites – frothed

1 teaspoon almond extract

1 cup slivered almonds

1 cup chopped red or green candied cherries (optional)

In a large bowl mix all the ingredients until well blended. Line a cookie tray with parchment paper and drop by ½ Tablespoon on the tray.

Bake for 25 minutes.

CRACKED CHOCOLATE COOKIES

Several years ago, Mom decided we should try to include something chocolate on our Christmas tray. We had never included chocolate cookies because I made a variety of chocolate candy (later in the book). These little chocolate cookies soon became a family favorite for special occasions.

Preheat oven to 375⁰

1 ¼ cups brown sugar packed

½ cup (1 cube) butter softened

½ cup Crisco

1 teaspoon vanilla

2 eggs

1 cup all-purpose flour

6 Tablespoons cocoa powder

½ teaspoon salt

½ teaspoon baking powder

2/3 cup *mini* chocolate chips

In a separate bowl mix flour, cocoa, salt, and baking powder and set aside.

In a bowl mix 1/3 cup sugar and ½ cup powdered sugar and set aside.

In a mixing bowl cream butter, Crisco, and sugars scraping bowl. Add vanilla and eggs. Add flour mixture and mix until well incorporated. Stir in chips.

Roll into 1-inch balls, roll in sugar/powdered sugar mixture

Bake 8-10 minutes. Cool on a wire rack.

CREAM CHEESE CHOCOLATE CHIP COOKIES

This is a softer version of the favorite chocolate chip cookie. There is one problem with this recipe, however. The cookie dough is so tasty you will have to refrain from eating too much or you may not have any cookies to bake.

Preheat oven to 350°

1 3 oz. package cream cheese softened

2 cubes butter softened

½ cup sugar

¾ cup brown sugar packed

1 egg

1 Tablespoon vanilla

2 cups all-purpose flour

2 teaspoons cornstarch

1 teaspoon baking soda

¼ teaspoon salt

1–12 oz. package semi-sweet chocolate chips

In a bowl mix flour, cornstarch, baking soda, and salt and set aside.

In a large mixing bowl cream butter, cream cheese and sugars until blended. Add egg and vanilla. Slowly mix in flour mixture and combine thoroughly. Stir in chips.

Drop cookies by teaspoon or Tablespoon on a cookie sheet lined with parchment paper.

Bake 10-12 minutes.

COWBOY COOKIES

This is a recipe from our dear friend Carmella Gyurko. This recipe makes 6 dozen cookies, perfect for a child's school party or if you are serving a crowd. Mom always said the recipe was easy because it calls for one cup of many things. You will need an extra-large baking bowl for this one!

Preheat oven to 350°

2 cubes butter softened

1 cup vegetable oil

1 cup brown sugar packed

1 egg

1 Tablespoon vanilla

½ teaspoon butter flavoring

1 teaspoon salt

1 teaspoon baking soda

1 teaspoon cream of tartar

1 cup Old Fashioned oatmeal

1 cup Rice Crispies cereal

1 cup coconut

1 cup chopped nuts

1 cup chocolate chips

In a *large* mixing bowl cream butter, oil, and sugars. Add eggs, vanilla, and butter flavor. Sift salt, soda, and cream of tartar into mixture mixing well. Stir in remaining ingredients.

Drop cookies on a parchment lined cookie sheet.

Bake 10-12 minutes.

Makes 6 dozen cookies.

Eleanor Gaccetta

"CUCIDATA" ITALIAN FILLED COOKIES

These are little bundles of fruit filling in a cream cheese crust. Growing up these were filled with a mixture of ground dates and figs. It is hard to say when the fruit filling began replacing the traditional mixture. The fruit filling is not store-bought jams and jellies, it must be purchased from a commercial bakery. This is a beautiful addition to any holiday cookie line up.

Preheat oven to 400°

Dough:

1 Tablespoon sugar
8 oz. cream cheese softened
2 ½ cups flour

Beat sugar, cream cheese and butter until well blended. Add flour and mix until a ball forms. On a floured surface, knead dough to thoroughly incorporate. Divide into 2 or 3 portions–cover with plastic wrap and refrigerate 3-4 hours.

Filling:

Option 1: Buy special baking jam from a commercial bakery like *Cakes by Karen*

Option 2: Combine:

½ lb. walnuts finely ground
1 cup sugar
½ cube melted butter

Line cookie sheets with parchment paper.

On a floured pastry mat roll dough into 8 x 8 sheet about 1/8 inch thick. With a pastry cutter (wheel) or sharp knife cut into 2x2 squares and fill with a small amount (1/2 teaspoon) of filling. Fold corners and tightly pinch closed.

Bake 17 minutes.

Dust with powder sugar to serve.

HELLO DOLLIES

This is a cookie bar recipe that was shared from a co-worker of mine during the 1980's and it quickly became a family favorite. This quick dessert to cut into bite sized squares and serves a crowd. It is hard to eat just one!

Preheat oven to 350^0

Made in one pan:

In an 8x8 or 9x9 baking pan:

Melt a cube of butter and pour 1 ½ cups graham cracker crumbs over the butter

Mix and press on the bottom of the pan.

Spread over the crumb mixture:

1 package chocolate chips

1 cup chopped walnuts or pecans

1 cup coconut

Pour a can of Eagle Brand sweetened condensed milk over the top of entire mixture.

Bake for 30 minutes.

Makes 3 dozen cookie bars.

Eleanor Gaccetta

HONEY COOKIES

This is a cornerstone Christmas cookie recipe in my mom's arsenal. This is the one cookie everyone waits to eat. It is a very time-consuming cookie to bake, fry and dip in honey. It must be made with the help of at least four people. After Mom was unable to bake, I began enlisting various members of the family to help at Christmas to bake these cookies. As time went on, the list of willing participants dwindled down to two cousins, Dorothy and Rosemary, and our friend, Lena. On a day near Christmas each year, we gathered at my home and spent a day baking upstairs and frying and honeying downstairs. Afterwards we sat for lunch and conversation. This recipe is a labor of love. This recipe makes enough cookies for all four families and their friends. My guess is that it makes at least 25 dozen cookies. Yes, you read that right.

12 eggs

1 cube butter melted and cooled

2 Tablespoons sugar

2 Tablespoons vanilla

7-8 cups all-purpose flour

Beat eggs, butter, sugar, and vanilla until smooth. Add 3 ½ cups flour, mix, and gradually add flour until a ball forms that is the consistency of pasta dough.

Roll the ball onto a floured surface, cut in half, and knead until it resembles pasta dough, about 10 minutes. Put in a plastic bag and let rest for 30 minutes.

With a sharp knife cut small rounds, flatten with the ball of your hand and coat with flour. Using the roller of a pasta machine attachment to a stand mixer, roll out the rounds using a medium-thin thickness. Cut diagonally with a pastry wheel making a slit in the middle of the strip. Pull one corner of the strip through the slit and continue this process with the remainder of the dough. Put the cookies on a towel-lined baking sheet.

Preheat 1 gallon of Vegetable or Canola oil to 350^0. Fry the cookies until slightly brown turning to cook both sides and place in a large container. Heat 1-36 oz. container of honey to a simmer in a large pan. Dip each cookie in the simmering honey and dry on wax paper for several hours before storing. These cookies can also be dusted with powder sugar.

NOTE: This recipe requires lots of utensils, pans, and hands. Cleanup is time consuming.

HONEY SAND BALLS

Preheat oven to 325^0

1 cup (2 cubes) butter softened

½ cup powdered sugar

2 Tablespoons honey

2 cups all-purpose flour

1 teaspoon vanilla

¼ teaspoon salt

¾ cup chopped walnuts or pecans

Cream butter and powdered sugar until smooth, add honey and vanilla and mix well. Add flour and salt incorporating thoroughly and stir in nuts.

Roll into 1-inch balls, place 1 ½ inches apart on a parchment lined cookie sheet.

Bake 14-16 minutes and dust with powdered sugar while warm.

JOHN'S SOFT CHOCOLATE CHIP COOKIES

I found this recipe for my Filipino brother when he asked if I had a recipe for soft chocolate chip cookies. John is unable to eat a lot of sugar, and I substituted with Monk sugar which is from sweet monk fruit. The results were surprising because they taste and bake the same as if using regular granulated sugar. I have made these for my own brother and other family members and think they are a worthy addition to this book.

Preheat oven to 325⁰

2 cups all-purpose flour

½ teaspoon baking soda

½ teaspoon salt

¾ cup butter melted

1 cup brown sugar packed

½ cup white sugar (or Monk fruit sugar)

1 egg

1 egg yolk

2 cups chocolate chips

Mix flour, baking soda and salt in a bowl and set aside.

In a bowl cream melted butter and sugars until creamy and add egg and egg yolk and mix well. Stir in the chocolate chips.

Drop by teaspoonful on a parchment lined cookie sheet leaving at least an inch in between.

Bake for 15 minutes.

Cookies will look a bit raw when they are removed from the oven; that is the texture you want.

Cool on wire rack.

ITALIAN KNOTS

Some Italian families bake these as traditional Easter and Christmas cookies. My mom, however, baked them year-round as coffee dunkers for my dad! Growing up on the farm, my dad would generally take a break in mid-afternoon (in the heat of the day) to have a cup of coffee and something sweet to tide him over until dinnertime. Mom made several different cookies, but Knots and Biscotti are the ones most often "dunked."

NOTE: This recipe can be doubled or cut in half.

Preheat oven to 400°

2 cubes butter softened

¾ cup sugar

1 Tablespoon vanilla

6 eggs

3 ½ cups all-purpose flour

4 teaspoons baking powder

Cream butter and sugar until mixed, add eggs and vanilla and mix until creamy. Add baking powder and flour in small quantities using a spoon. Frequently scrape the bowl with a spatula. The dough should be soft.

On a floured surface roll a handful of dough into the shape of a rope. Cut into lengths that will allow dough to be braided, or twisted into a knot, or left whole. Line cookie sheets with parchment paper and place the cookies about ½ inch apart.

Bake 12-15 minutes.

If these are made for a special occasion, they are generally frosted with a mixture of powdered sugar and milk.

LEMON COOKIES

This is a favorite cookie of my brother, Don. After our mother passed-away, I would make these for him often upon request. Don is never shy about asking me to bake cakes or cookies as he observes the afternoon tradition of stopping and having a cup of coffee and something sweet. I am always happy to ensure he is satisfied.

Preheat oven to 350^0

1 ¾ cup all-purpose flour

½ teaspoon baking soda

½ teaspoon salt

1 ½ Tablespoons lemon zest

1 cube butter

1 cup sugar

1 egg

1 teaspoon vanilla

2 Tablespoons lemon juice

Mix flour, baking soda, salt, and lemon zest in a bowl and set aside.

Cream butter and sugar until smooth scraping bowl often. Add egg, vanilla, and lemon juice and combine thoroughly. Add flour mixture slowly and mix until incorporated.

Drop by the teaspoonful onto a cookie sheet lined with parchment paper.

Bake 12-14 minutes.

LEMON RICOTTA COOKIES

This is a full-bodied lemon cookie that delights the palate. After receiving the "naked" ricotta cookie, a cousin told me she uses lemon zest and lemon juice for a variation that her family enjoys. I make this cookie for Christmas and if I am asked to bring cookies to neighborhood parties or family gatherings. It makes several dozen cookies and is always a crowd pleaser! The lemon taste is always refreshing.

Preheat oven to 375°

2 cubes butter
2 cups sugar
1 15 oz. container ricotta cheese
2 Tablespoons lemon juice (juice of 2 large lemons)
2 eggs
4 cups all-purpose flour
2 Tablespoons baking powder
2 Tablespoons lemon zest

In a bowl mix flour, baking powder, and lemon zest and set aside.

In a mixing bowl cream butter and sugar until blended, scraping bowl often. Add ricotta cheese, lemon juice and eggs and mix thoroughly. Slowly incorporate flour mixture and mix until a soft dough forms scraping bowl often.

Using a small ice cream scoop drop onto a parchment lined baking sheet.

Bake 12-15 minutes. Cool.

Dip top of cookie into a light frosting:

Frosting:

2-3 cups powdered sugar
2 Tablespoons lemon juice
2 Tablespoons lemon zest
1 teaspoon milk

MALTED MILK SHORTBREAD COOKIES

Malted milk reminds me of when we were growing up and Mom would make milkshakes because my father loved ice cream. Malted milk powder is easy to add to recipes and it gives this shortbread cookie a distinctive taste. This is an easy cookie to make. Make a batch and put them in your cookie jar for a treat when your sweet tooth calls.

Preheat oven to 350^0

2 cubes butter softened

1 cup powdered sugar

2 Tablespoons Malted Milk powder

½ teaspoon salt

½ teaspoon vanilla

2 cups all-purpose flour

Cream butter, sugar, and malted milk powder until smooth. Scrape bowl and add remaining ingredients until dough forms soft ball.

This dough can be shaped in a flat cylinder to be rolled out and cut into shapes or shaped into a log to be sliced. Either way the dough should be refrigerated for 3 hours.

Slice logs into ¼ inch cookies and place on a parchment lined cookie sheet.

Roll flat cylinders on a floured surface until ¼ inch thick. Cut with a cookie cutter. Re-use dough and continue rolling until all the dough is used.

Bake 20-30 minutes.

Eleanor Gaccetta

MOCHA LOGS

This cookie recipe was shared by Carmella Gyurko who is a wonderful friend and baker! I have made these cookies as part of my Christmas trays for several years. They are a small one-bite coffee-chocolate cookie that disappears from the tray quickly. Mom liked them because they were a new addition to our usual Christmas fare.

Preheat oven to 375^0

1 cup (2 cubes) butter softened

3 Tablespoons instant coffee

¾ cup sugar

1 egg

1 teaspoon vanilla

2 ¼ cups all-purpose flour

½ teaspoon salt

¼ teaspoon baking powder

1 6 oz. package semi-sweet chips

1 cup walnuts

Mix flour, salt, and baking powder in a bowl and set aside.

Cream butter, sugar, and coffee until mixed scraping the bowl often. Add eggs and vanilla, and scrape bowl. Add flour mixture gradually until well blended. Stir in the semi-sweet chips and nuts.

Line cookie sheet with parchment paper.

On a floured surface, roll dough into 2 ½ inch logs.

Bake 8-12 minutes.

(NAKED) RICOTTA COOKIES

This is a simple vanilla pillow of a cookie that delights the palate. This cookie recipe came to me when baking for a cousin's son's wedding. We frosted them with the colors of the wedding party. I make this and other variations of this cookie (in this book) for Christmas. I also bake them for neighborhood parties or family gatherings. Whether you make this cookie "naked," lemon, or chocolate flavored, it is sure to be a crowd pleaser. The recipe makes several dozen cookies.

Preheat oven to 375⁰

2 cubes butter
2 cups sugar
1-15 oz. container ricotta cheese
2 eggs
4 cups all-purpose flour
2 Tablespoons baking powder
1 Tablespoon vanilla

In a bowl mix flour and baking powder and set aside.

In a mixing bowl cream butter and sugar until blended, scraping bowl often. Add ricotta cheese, vanilla and eggs and mix thoroughly. Slowly incorporate flour mixture and mix until a soft dough forms, scraping bowl often.

Using a small ice cream scoop, drop onto a parchment lined baking sheet.

Bake 12-15 minutes.
Cool.
Dip top of cookie into a light frosting:

Frosting:

2-3 cups powdered sugar
2-3 Tablespoons milk
1 Tablespoon vanilla

AUNT JENNIE'S OATMEAL COOKIES

My Aunt Jennie (Mom's sister-in-law) was a wonderful baker. In fact, her daughter, Anna Marie, and I used to wish we had a fraction of the money we spent for years on butter, eggs, sugar, and flour so they could experiment baking in the kitchen. There was always some new recipe one of them would want to try. They would laugh and enjoy time together in the kitchen for hours on end. Sometimes their efforts were successful and sometimes not. Let it be known that when a recipe failed it was always because someone left something out or didn't share the correct recipe. Annie and I always had fun while they baked because we would slip away and go shopping, to the movies, or play a round of golf. By the way, this recipe is long and time consuming but good in the end!

Preheat oven to 375^0

½ cup raisins

½ cup boiling water

¾ cup shortening

1 ½ cups sugar

2 eggs

1 teaspoon vanilla

2 ½ cups all-purpose flour

1 teaspoon baking powder

1 teaspoon baking soda

1 teaspoon salt

1 heaping teaspoon cinnamon

½ teaspoon cloves

2 cups rolled oats

1 cup chocolate chips

1 cup chopped dates

1 cup dried cranberries

1 cup chopped walnuts

1. Soak raisins in boiling water until plumped. Set aside and drain water.

2. In a bowl sift flour, baking powder, baking soda, salt, cinnamon, and cloves, and set aside.

3. Mix dates, cranberries, chocolate chips, and nuts with a bit of flour to prevent sticking.

4. Cream shortening, eggs, sugar, and vanilla. Add date mixture and mix. Scrape bowl. Add raisins, rolled oats, and flour mixture. Scrape bowl and mix until thoroughly combined.

Line cookie sheets with parchment paper. Drop cookies 2 inches apart.

Bake 9-10 minutes.

Cool on wire rack.

REGULAR OATMEAL COOKIES

I'm sure after reading the previous recipe for Aunt Jennie's Oatmeal Cookies. you may be hesitant to attempt that level of a challenge. Try this one.

Preheat oven to 375⁰

2 cubes butter softened

¼ cup sugar

¾ cups light brown sugar firmly packed

1 package instant vanilla pudding

2 eggs

1 ¼ cups all-purpose flour

1 teaspoon baking soda

3 ½ cups rolled oats

½ cup raisins (optional)

Mix flour and baking soda and set aside.

Cream butter and sugars until smooth, add pudding mix and eggs and beat until smooth. Scrape the bowl, add flour mixture, and mix thoroughly. Stir in the oats and raisins.

Line cookie sheets with parchment paper. Drop by the rounded teaspoonful on the cookie sheet.

Bake 10-12 minutes.

PECAN CUTOUT COOKIES

This recipe can be halved easily.

Preheat oven to 350°

2 cups pecan halves

1 cup sugar divided

2 cups all-purpose flour

1 cup (2 cubes) butter softened

Using a food processor finely grind pecans.

In a large bowl add pecans, ½ cup sugar, and flour. Cut in butter until you have pea-sized crumbs.

Transfer to a clean work surface and gently knead to form a ball. This dough is dry, and it will take time to come together so be patient. Cut ball in half.

On a lightly floured surface roll dough to ¼ inch thickness and cut with a pastry wheel or knife.

Bake 10 minutes.

Vanilla sugar mixture for after baking cookies:

2/3 cup sugar

½ teaspoon vanilla

Dip warm cookies in vanilla sugar and cool on a rack.

PECAN FINGERS

This is a shortbread cookie. This recipe calls for the baked cookie to be rolled in powdered sugar. An option for a Halloween treat is to form an indentation "fingernail" on top of each log and dip one end into melted white chocolate colored red with food coloring.

Preheat oven to 325^0

1 cup (2 cubes) butter softened

¼ cup powdered sugar

1 Tablespoon vanilla

1 Tablespoon water

2 cups flour

½ teaspoon salt

2 cups chopped pecans

Powdered sugar

In a mixing bowl cream butter and sugar until mixed scraping bowl. Add vanilla, water, and salt mixing thoroughly. Incorporate flour and nuts. Roll dough in plastic wrap and chill 1 hour.

Pinch off pieces of dough and form into small rolls the size of a finger. Line cookie sheets with parchment paper and line the trays with the "fingers."

Bake for 12-14 minutes.

Roll in powdered sugar while warm.

PECAN SANDIE COOKIES

This is one of the family's favorite cookies. Cookies of all varieties were baked before store bought cookies began appearing in the cookie jars. Mom decided to try this shortbread cookie as an alternative to buying a package of Pecan Sandies from the grocery store. The cookie is a wonderful addition for holidays, group gatherings, or special occasions. It is easy to make, easy to eat. It becomes a favorite quickly and one people do not soon forget.

This recipe can be halved.

Preheat oven to 350°

1 pound (4 cubes) butter softened

1 1/12 cups powdered sugar

1 teaspoon *Kosher* salt

2 Tablespoons vanilla

4 cups all-purpose flour

2 cups toasted pecans–chopped

In a small frying pan toast the pecans on medium heat and set aside.

In a large mixing bowl cream butter and powdered sugar, add vanilla and salt and mix well. Scrape bowl slowly adding flour and mix until it is incorporated. Scrape bowl often. Stir in nuts.

Make several cylinder-shaped logs. Wrap with plastic wrap and refrigerate for 3 hours.

Slice logs into ¼ inch thickness. Line cookie sheets with parchment paper and arrange cookies close together (not touching).

Bake 12-14 minutes until lightly brown on the bottom.

Store in an airtight container.

NOTE: The cylinders can be wrapped in plastic wrap and then double foil and then frozen to be baked later. Thaw the dough in the refrigerator, slice, and bake.

PIZZELLES

This is the quintessential waffle cookie made with a traditional pizzella cooker. While growing up, my mother had a pizzella iron that made one cookie at a time over the open flame of a gas stove. (I still have it.) A double batch of this recipe (which is generally what is made for Christmas holidays) yields up to 12 dozen cookies. Imagine the hours it took to make a batch one cookie at a time, but that is how it was done back in the day. Today, I have pizzelles nearly year-round in the cookie box. My nephews will often bring the cookie box to the kitchen and eat pizzelles over the kitchen sink, so crumbs do not go on the floor. One of my nieces has learned to make gluten-free pizzelles for her husband. My mother's recipe below is a keeper! Invest in an iron and enjoy.

6 eggs

2 cubes butter softened

1 Tablespoon vanilla or anise

1 1/3 cups sugar

2-2 ½ cups all-purpose flour

In a large mixing bowl, Cream butter and sugar until fluffy, add eggs and flavoring. Add flour a little at a time, scraping bowl often. Batter should stay on a spoon but not be stiff. If the batter is too stiff cookies will be hard.

Always spray the pizzella iron with non-stick spray before warming for 5 minutes. Bake cookies according to the manufacturer's instructions.

Makes 5-6 dozen cookies.

PUMPKIN COOKIES

This recipe is from my late sister-in-law, Connie. Connie's mother would bake these cookies in the fall, and they disappeared as fast as they came out of the oven. My mom always looked forward to Connie sharing her Pumpkin cookies. Today my three nieces bake these cookies for their families, and I know this recipe will stay in the family for many generations to come.

Preheat oven to 350⁰

2 cups sugar

2 cups shortening (can be part butter)

2 eggs

2 cups canned pumpkin

1 Tablespoon vanilla

4 cups all-purpose flour

1 teaspoon baking powder

1 teaspoon baking soda

½ teaspoon salt

1 package chocolate chips

1 teaspoon pumpkin pie spice (optional)

Mix flour, baking powder, baking soda, salt, and spice, and set aside.

In a mixing bowl, cream sugar and shortening. Add eggs, vanilla, and pumpkin and mix thoroughly. Gradually add flour mixture scraping bowl often. Stir in chocolate chips.

Line cookie sheets with parchment paper and drop by teaspoon leaving one inch between cookies.

Bake 15-18 minutes.

SHORTBREAD COOKIE BARS WITH SALTED CARAMEL

This recipe is best baked in a cast iron skillet. If you do not have a cast iron skillet, be sure the skillet being used is oven proof up to 350⁰.

Preheat oven to 350⁰

Shortbread:

2 cubes butter softened

½ cup powdered sugar

½ teaspoon salt

2 ¼ cups all-purpose flour

½ teaspoon baking powder

Mix salt, flour and baking powder in a bowl and set aside.

Cream butter and powdered sugar until creamy, scraping bowl. Add flour mixture and mix thoroughly. Mixture will form a ball of dough.

Press into a cast iron skillet or oven proof skillet. Prick top generously with a fork and score to make wedges. Bake for 25 minutes. Remove from oven and cool.

Caramel:

½ cup heavy cream

20 caramel candies

½ teaspoon vanilla

Sea Salt

Melt caramel candies in the cream over medium heat in a saucepan. Once the mixture is creamy remove from the heat and add vanilla. Pour over cooled cookies, drizzle with sea salt and return to the oven for 15 minutes.

Store in an airtight container.

PIONEER WOMAN SUGAR COOKIES

This recipe is a variation from traditional sugar cookies which are rolled and cut out with cookie cutters. The recipe can be cut in half.

Preheat oven to 350^0

2 cubes butter softened

1 cup vegetable oil

1 cup sugar

1 cup powdered sugar

1 Tablespoon vanilla

2 eggs

4 cups, plus 2 Tablespoons all-purpose flour

1 teaspoon baking powder

1 teaspoon baking soda

1 teaspoon salt

Mix flour, baking powder, baking soda, and salt in a bowl and set aside.

In a mixing bowl cream butter, sugars, vanilla, oil, and eggs together. Scrape the bowl often. Gradually add the dry ingredients. Dough will be soft. Refrigerate one hour.

Line cookie sheets with parchment paper. Using a small 1-inch scoop make small balls and place one inch apart on cookie sheet. Coat the bottom of a glass with sugar and butter and press each ball slightly. Dip the glass in sugar for each cookie.

Bake 10-15 minutes until slightly brown.

Eleanor Gaccetta

ROSETTES

This recipe comes from our wonderful friend, Carmella Gyurko. Rosettes are a traditional holiday cookie made with a special iron. The dough must rest for 2 hours on the counter before frying. My mother tried rosette recipes from various relatives and bought several irons. This was still not one of her more successful cookies to make. Mama Mel's recipe is different.

To maintain temperature of the oil for frying it is recommended that they be fried in an electric frying pan.

2 eggs

2 teaspoons sugar

¼ teaspoon salt

1 cup milk

3 teaspoons lemon extract

1 cup sifted all-purpose flour.

Vegetable or Canola oil for frying

Beat eggs, sugar, salt, milk, and lemon together until blended. Add sifted flour and mix. The mixture should be the consistency of heavy cream. Let stand on counter for 2 hours.

Add oil to electric frying pan and heat to 370^0-375^0.

Dip clean rosette iron in the hot oil until heated. Dip hot iron into the batter. Lower iron back into the oil for 30 seconds. Using a knife loosen the edges of the cookie and let it fry. Drain on paper towels.

Pack in airtight container with paper towels between layers.

Drizzle with honey or dust with powdered sugar to serve.

Makes 2 dozen cookies.

RUM BALLS

This is a Christmas recipe from my cousin, Elizabeth Talarico. Liz makes these little no-bake cookies for her family and friends for the holidays. The men in the family would enjoy popping these little treats while playing cards during holiday gatherings.

2 ½ cups graham cracker crumbs

2 Tablespoons cocoa powder

1 cup walnuts finely chopped

3 Tablespoons corn syrup

½ cup dark rum or bourbon

1 cup powdered sugar

Measure graham cracker crumbs, cocoa powder, nuts, corn syrup and alcohol in a bowl and mix thoroughly. Using a 1-inch scoop or large melon-baller, roll into balls. Roll in powdered sugar and store in an air-tight container. Use waxed paper between layers.

These can be frozen.

SCRUPEDS

This is the naked version of the honey cookie with a slight variation in the recipe. This cookie is generally dusted with powdered sugar after it is fried. My mom made a mountain of these cookies when I was growing up during the holiday season. They would be on the platter between the honey cookies and pizzelles (3 distinct tastes). Then decorated spritz, butter cookies, filled cookies, and sesame cookies rounded out that platter. Like the other recipes from her era, this makes many dozens of cookies.

½ cube butter melted

8 eggs

¼ cup sugar

1 ½ Tablespoons vanilla

1 Tablespoon bourbon (optional)

5 cups all-purpose flour

Vegetable or Canola oil for frying

In a large mixing bowl, combine butter, eggs, sugar, vanilla, and bourbon until smooth. Gradually add the flour until the dough is the consistency of pasta dough and a ball forms.

Place dough on a floured surface and knead until the dough is smooth and elastic. Cut the ball in half and wrap in plastic wrap.

Using the roller on a pasta machine, cut small rounds of dough, flatten and flour. Run through the roller of the pasta machine using a medium thickness. Cut into strips with a pastry wheel making a slit in the middle and pulling one corner through the slit.

Heat oil in a large pan to 375° and dry cookies a few at a time turning to brown on both sides.

Drain on paper towels and dust with powdered sugar before serving. Store in a dry place in a covered container.

SESAME SEED COOKIES

This is a traditional Sicilian cookie. My mother's father was from Sicily. Her mother was from the southern part of the "boot" from the villages of Calabria and Potenza, as were my father's parents. Consequently, and the bulk of the recipes in this book are made with southern Italian roots. This recipe makes a small mountain of cookies. I vividly remember watching a group of ladies sitting around a huge bowl of dough. They would simply pinch a tiny amount of dough from the bowl, roll it into a small cylinder, and repeat dozens of times. The cookies were rolled into a pan of sesame seeds prior to cooking. Because the recipe calls for 6 teaspoons of baking powder these little gems will puff up, so leave a good amount of space between them when baking. This is a good cookie.

Preheat oven to 375^0

3 cubes of butter softened

1 ½ cups sugar

6 eggs

1 Tablespoon vanilla

1 Tablespoon orange flavoring

6 cups all-purpose flour

6 teaspoons baking powder

2 cups hulled sesame seeds toasted

2 teaspoons milk

Mix flour and baking powder in a bowl and set aside.

In a large mixing bowl cream butter and sugar until fluffy. Add eggs 2 at a time beating thoroughly, add vanilla and orange flavorings. Add half the flour mixture incorporating thoroughly before adding the remaining mixture.

Place sesame seeds in a cake pan and coat with a small amount of milk.

Pinch off small amounts of dough, roll into a small cylinder and roll in the seeds to coat.

Line cookie sheets with parchment paper. Leave space between the cookies as they will double in size as they bake. Bake 12-17 minutes. Store in airtight container. These can be frozen.

SNICKERDOODLES

This is an after-school cookie most kids love. It is a variation of a shortbread cookie that is rolled in cinnamon sugar. My mother did not bake this cookie on a regular basis, but it was always a treat when she did.

Preheat oven to 350^0

2 cubes butter softened

1 cup sugar

1 teaspoon vanilla

½ teaspoon cinnamon

2 cups all-purpose flour

1 teaspoon salt

In a small bowl mix and set aside:

1/3 cup sugar

½ teaspoon cinnamon

Cream butter and sugar until fluffy, scraping bowl often. Add vanilla, cinnamon, flour, and salt in small batches mixing thoroughly. Mix until a soft ball forms.

Roll into logs 2 inches in diameter and wrap in plastic wrap. Refrigerate 3 hours.

Line cookie sheets with parchment paper. Slice cookies ¼ inch thick and roll in cinnamon-sugar before baking.

Bake 20-25 minutes.

Eleanor Gaccetta

SPRITZ COOKIES

This is the buttery vanilla-flavored cookie that won the heart of my grandfather after my dad married my mother. My mom would bake a 5-gallon container of these cookies weekly for the men to enjoy when they had afternoon coffee on the farm. This cookie is made with a special cookie press that has numerous attachments to make cookies shaped from Christmas trees to cookie bars. Know that it does take a certain amount of skill to operate this press. A fun cookie for anytime or any season.

Preheat oven to 375

4 cubes (1-pound) butter softened

2 cups sugar

2 eggs

5 teaspoons vanilla

1 teaspoon salt

5 cups all-purpose flour

Cream butter and sugar until fluffy, scraping bowl frequently. Add eggs, vanilla, and salt. Slowly incorporate the flour to make a soft dough.

Line cookie sheets with parchment paper and follow directions to use the cookie press and make cookies.

Bake 10 minutes.

Store in an air-tight container.

Depending upon the size cookie, this may make up to 5 or 6 dozen cookies.

SWEET BUTTER COOKIES

Aka Melt-aways

This is a cornerstone in my mom's and my Christmas cookie lineup. This is also a staple when making cookies for weddings or other large, special gatherings. My mother got this recipe from her aunt, Beatrice Belmonte, who lived in Milwaukee, Wisconsin. One holiday season she shared this recipe with my mother and taught her how to bake it with love. My mother shared the recipe with other relatives, but no one ever perfected the art of baking this cookie as my mother did. I have baked this cookie alongside my mother since I was a teenager and am one of the only ones who can make it like she did. Mom called these crescent cookies because they are formed in the shape of a crescent (half-moon). They are called Melt-aways because they will melt in your mouth at first bite if made right!

Preheat oven to 350^0

4 cubes (1-pound) butter softened

½ cup powdered sugar

¼ cup granulated sugar

4 egg yolks

1 Tablespoon almond flavoring

3-3 ½ cups all-purpose flour

Powdered Sugar

Cream butter and sugar until smooth and fluffy. Scrape the bowl often with a spatula. Add egg yolks and almond and beat until mixed. Add flour in small amounts until thoroughly mixed. Dough should be soft enough to hold together when rolled into a cylinder.

NOTE: Too much flour in this dough will result in a tough cookie.

On a lightly floured surface break small amounts of dough and roll into a rope about ½ inch thick. Cut into ½ inch pieces and roll into a crescent shape. This is a small cookie.

Line cookie tins with parchment paper and place cookies close to each other.

Bake 15-18 minutes or until the edges are slightly brown.

Do not overcook. Cool completely.

Line an airtight container with waxed paper cutting several additional sheets to place between layers of cookies.

Using a coffee strainer, dust the bottom of the waxed paper with powdered sugar, line with a

layer of cookies and liberally dust the tops and sides of the cookies with powdered sugar. Repeat until all the cookies are covered in powdered sugar.

Store in an air-tight container.

This recipe can be frozen.

This recipe will net 10 dozen small cookies.

SWEET BUTTER COOKIE ALTERNATIVES

Remember, Mom always said, "A lady always loves to have options." The sweet butter cookie recipe is versatile. Here are a few alternative recipes that can be made from the previous sweet butter cookie.

Preheat oven to 350^0

Thumbprint Cookies

Make the sweet butter cookie recipe.

In a separate bowl add ½ cup chopped nuts or toasted coconut.

Set aside a jar of orange marmalade or your favorite jam.

Bake the dough following the recipe. Roll into 1-inch balls and roll in nuts or coconut.

Line cookie sheets with parchment paper and place balls onto the sheet. Make a small indentation or "well" in the top with your thumb.

Bake 12 minutes, remove from oven, and add marmalade or jam in the indentation. Return to the oven and bake 5 more minutes. Cool on a wire rack.

Snowballs

Make sweet butter cookie recipe. Stir 1 cup chopped walnuts or pecans to dough.

Roll into 1-inch balls and place on cookie sheets lined with parchment paper. Bake 12-18 minutes. Roll in powdered sugar when cool and store.

Chocolate Butter Cookies

Make sweet butter cookie recipe, substituting ¼ cup cocoa powder for all purpose flour. This cookie can be rolled into balls or made into crescent shapes. Dust cookies with a combination of powdered sugar and cocoa powder when cooled.

SOUR CREAM TWISTS

One Christmas my friend's mother, Elaine, and my mother swapped their favorite Christmas recipes. Mrs. Accamasso's family was from northern Italy and they cooked very differently from my mother's Sicilian family. Those two ladies shared a wonderful friendship as Elaine and I still do. They would be delighted to know the other was baking her cookies for a Christmas tray.

Preheat oven to 375°

3 ½ cups all-purpose flour

1 teaspoon salt

1 cup shortening–part butter

1 package dry rapid rise yeast

¼ cup warm water

¾ cup sour cream

1 whole egg, plus 2 egg yolks beaten

2 teaspoons vanilla

1 cup sugar to roll dough

In a large mixing bowl sift flour and salt, cut in shortening until pea size pieces form. Dissolve yeast in warm water and add to the flour mixture. Add sour cream, eggs, and vanilla. Using a dough hook mix into a soft dough. When a soft ball forms cover with a damp cloth and refrigerate 2 hours.

Divide into 2 or 3 balls and roll on a *sugared* pastry mat. Roll into an oblong shape dusting with sugar until ¼ thickness. Using a pastry wheel or sharp knife cut into strips. Twist the ends in opposite directions several times and place on a parchment lined cookie sheet.

Bake 15 minutes.

Remove from baking sheet and cool on a wire rack.

ULTIMATE CHOCOLATE CHIP COOKIES

Preheat oven to 375⁰

¾ cup (1 ½ cubes) butter softened

1 ¼ cups brown sugar firmly packed

2 Tablespoons milk

1 Tablespoon vanilla

1 egg

1 ¾ cups all-purpose flour

1 teaspoon salt

¾ teaspoon baking soda

1 cup (1small bag) chocolate chips

1 cup pecan pieces

In a bowl mix flour, salt and baking soda and set aside.

In a mixing bowl cream butter and sugar until fluffy, scraping the bowl. Add milk, vanilla and the egg and mix thoroughly. Gradually add the flour mixture, scraping the bowl frequently until incorporated. Stir in the chocolate chips and nuts.

Line 2 cookie sheets with parchment paper. Spoon dough by the Tablespoon and leave 3 inches of space between cookies.

Bake 8-10 minutes for chewy cookies.

Bake 12-14 minutes for crisp cookies.

Eleanor Gaccetta

WALNUT HORN COOKIES

Preheat oven to 325⁰

Preheat oven to 325^0

1 cup (2 cubes) plus 1 Tablespoon butter softened

8 oz. cream cheese softened

½ cup milk

1 teaspoon milk

3 cups all-purpose flour

1/8 teaspoon salt

4 cups walnuts grated

1 ¼ cups sugar divided

Dough:

Cream 2 cubes butter and cream cheese until fluffy. Add flour and mix until a ball forms.

Filling:

Melt remaining butter, combine walnuts, ¾ cup sugar, milk, vanilla, and salt in a large bowl.

On a floured surface, roll dough into a circle, cut into wedges, and spread nut mixture onto wedges. Roll wedges into crescents starting with the wide end.

Bake 35-40 minutes until lightly brown.

Roll each crescent in sugar while warm.

Cook on a wire rack.

Makes 4 dozen.

WHIPPED SPRITZ COOKIES

This is a simple, six ingredient recipe that produces a tasty treat. This recipe was discovered (by me) after a disastrous outing with the spritz cookie press. My mom would always say some days it is best not to bake. It was not unusual that at least one-time during holiday season when baking that an entire batch of dough or cookies would go into the waste basket as a failure. Even the most skilled bakers and cooks have bad days. This easy cookie will bring a smile to your day.

Preheat oven to 350⁰

2 cubes butter softened

2 teaspoons vanilla

1 cup powdered sugar

1 1/3 cups all-purpose flour

¼ cup cornstarch

½ teaspoon sea salt

Mix flour, cornstarch and sea salt in a bowl and set aside.

Cream the butter and powdered sugar until smooth, add vanilla and mix thoroughly. Slowly incorporate flour mixture until a soft ball forms.

Using a 1-inch cookie scoop, make balls and place 1-inch apart on a cookie sheet lined with parchment paper. Using a fork dipped in flour flatten the balls and make and indentation.

Bake 8-10 minutes.

WINE COOKIES

This is a traditional Italian cookie that was served for the holidays. There are many variations of this recipe. My mother improvised this recipe by taking a bit of this and that from the recipes of her dear friends Ella Dodaro and Nettie Scarpello. These cookies are generally rolled on a board with deep grooves to give them air and a shape. Nettie's husband, Frank, made the boards for all the women his wife knew who baked wine cookies! This is a cookie that is best consumed the same day it is baked. The honey will crystalize into the dough and the cookie will be hard. But while it is fresh, it is super.

1 cup Muscatel wine
½ cup Wesson oil
2 eggs
½ cup sugar
4 cups all-purpose flour
2 teaspoons baking powder
Pinch of salt
Wesson oil to fry
Honey for dipping
Chopped nuts (optional)
Mix flour, sugar, baking powder, and salt in a bowl and set aside.
In a large mixing bowl beat wine, oil, eggs, and sugar until well blended.
Dough will be soft.
Heat oil to 350⁰.

Roll into small balls and roll over grooves of a special board or a lightly over cheese grater to put air into the cookie. Fry the cookies in small batches and drain on waxed paper.

Heat honey in a deep saucepan on low heat and dip cookies in honey and drain on parchment paper. Optional to roll in chopped nuts while warm.

CANDY

Candy–the ultimate sweet confectionary treat. Making candy is truly an art of love and patience. Making candy can be fun and is always a wonderful addition to any cookie tray or sweet lineup. Enjoy!

GENERATIONS 5 AND 6

Don and Connie's Family

Pam and Tony with children Cody (Hannah), McKayla and Isabella

Lori and Andy with children Drew and Austin

Bobbi and Jimmy with children Brooklyn, Spencer, Brailee, Paislee, and James

Eleanor Gaccetta

ANGEL KISSES

Angel kisses are a lovely meringue cookie. Mom would make these when she had a recipe that called for egg yolks (sweet butter cookies) and the whites would be staring at her from the cup on the counter. These are airy and light. You will note there is an optional method for meringue shells at the end of the Angel Kisses recipe!

Preheat oven to 200^0

2 egg whites

4 teaspoons cream of tartar

Pinch of salt

½ cup plus 1 Tablespoon sugar

Beat egg whites and cream of tartar until stiff. Slowly add salt and sugar continue beating.

Line cookie sheets with parchment paper. Pipe with a pastry bag or drop by teaspoons unto tray. These should be about the size of a chocolate kiss candy. Bake for 1 ½ hours (90 minutes). Turn oven off and leave "kisses" in the oven for 4 hours.

Leave them in the oven so the meringue dries.

NOTE: This recipe can also be spooned into a 3-inch round with a well in the middle. Bake the same as above. When cool, serve with fresh fruit in the well and top with whipped cream.

CHERRY CREAM CHEESE CANDY

This is a holiday candy from our dear friend, Carmella Gyruko. This confectionary requires a couple of days from preparation to finish. I began making this candy for my Christmas cookie tray which eventually became a candy tray for Christmas. One reasons I began making candy is for the gluten-free members of my family. This recipe can easily be doubled or tripled.

Day 1:

½ cup powdered sugar

½ cup slivered almonds

½ cup candied cherries

½ teaspoon almond extract

1 8 oz. package cream cheese softened

Cream the cream cheese, sugar, and almond extract. Stir in almonds and cherries. Chill in refrigerator 2 hours.

Using a melon-baller, roll into balls and line on a baking sheet lined with parchment paper.

Freeze overnight.

Day 2:

1 6 oz. package white chocolate

1 Tablespoon vegetable oil

Melt the chocolate and vegetable oil in a double boiler. Dip balls in white chocolate and place on waxed paper lined cookie sheets. Refrigerate 1 hour.

Store in air-tight container with waxed paper between layers.

CHOCOLATE PEANUT CLUSTERS

My mom made at least a ton of peanut clusters when we were growing up during the fall and winter months. When the weather was cooler, the chocolate would not melt or get rancid. There was always a container of peanut clusters in the cabinet. Today, I make these for my brother who hides them from his grandkids in the pantry. Although they are peanut clusters, I have made them with mixed nuts, cashews, and pecans. Be sure the nuts are salted and dry roasted.

1 12 oz. package semi-sweet chocolate chips

1 12 oz. package milk chocolate chips

12 oz. white chocolate coarsely chopped

5 cups salted dry roasted peanuts

NOTE: Can substitute pecans, cashews, or mixed nuts

In a heavy saucepan over low heat, stir chocolate chips and white chocolate until melted and smooth. Remove from heat and stir in nuts.

Line baking sheets with waxed paper and drop nuts and chocolate by the Tablespoon. Put in a cool place or refrigerate until firm. Makes 10 dozen.

Option: Melt candy and chips in a double-boiler over low heat stirring until smooth. Remove from the heat and stir in nuts. Drop by Tablespoon onto a cookie sheet lined with waxed paper.

Put waxed paper between layers and store in an air-tight container.

CREAM CHEESE CANDIES

These are the little mints that look like wedding bells or baby booties and were always on a tray at a wedding or baby shower. It was hard not to grab the tray, sit down, and eat them all! You can purchase molds with various shapes of bells, booties, and animals that the mixture is flattened into. This recipe is a simple addition to the holiday lineup.

3 oz. cream cheese

¼ teaspoon peppermint or almond extract

3 cups powdered sugar

Colored sugar (optional)

Mix cream cheese and extract until well blended. Beat in ½ sugar and blend. Knead in the remaining sugar.

Shape into ½ inch balls or you can roll in colored sugar.

Line cookie sheets with waxed paper and place the balls onto the paper. Flatten balls with a fork.

Let stand 1-2 hours.

Store between layers of waxed paper in an air-tight container in the refrigerator.

COCONUT JOYS

This is one of the favorite candies on my Christmas line-up. If you love coconut, this is the homemade version of a naked Mounds! When I was caring for Mom, my brother would always manage to visit the day he knew I was making this candy. He would sit at the breakfast bar watching or keep coming into the kitchen to grab another candy from the tray. Just remembering those visits still makes me smile.

This recipe can be doubled or tripled

1 ½ cups flaked coconut

½ cup powdered sugar

½ cup (1/2 cube) melted butter

2 Tablespoons pecans chopped

Pulse coconut in a food processor to reduce the length of the flakes. (optional)

Line cookie trays with waxed paper or parchment paper.

In a large bowl combine all the ingredients. Make 1-inch balls and place on a prepared cookie tray. Chill for 1 hour in refrigerator.

Store in airtight container with waxed paper between the layers.

DATE BALLS

This recipe was shared by Carmella Gyruko from her Christmas line-up. I began making this candy when I needed to find a gluten-free alternative for my nephew, Tony. This is a wonderful addition to any holiday tray and provides a variation with the dates. Spoiler alert–this is a very messy candy to roll.

Preheat oven to 350°

2 eggs

2 Tablespoons sugar

1 cup cut up dates

1 cup flaked coconut

1 cup nuts chopped (pecans or walnuts)

1 teaspoon vanilla

¼ teaspoon almond extract

Sugar for coating

In a large mixing bowl beat eggs and sugar until mixed well. Mix dates, coconut, nuts, vanilla, and almond until well blended.

Spray bottom and sides of a 2-quart casserole dish with non-stick spray.

Turn mixture into the dish and spread evenly.

Bake 30 minutes.

Remove from oven and beat with a wooden spoon–yes, beat the hell out of it!

Cool. Roll into 1-inch balls and roll in sugar to coat.

Store in air-tight container with waxed paper between the layers.

EASY FUDGE

Fudge is the quintessential holiday candy. As with other things in my cookbook, there are four options for fudge in this section to choose from. My mother made every conceivable fudge recipe that was ever printed. She was always looking for something different and the amount of work expended on the recipe was never a consideration.

This recipe is for one 9x9 square pan. If the recipe is doubled, use a 9x13 pan.

Line a 9x9 square pan with waxed paper or aluminum foil leaving 2 inches above the sides. Spray with non-stick spray.

3 cups chocolate chips (semi-sweet or dark)

1-14 oz. can Eagle Brand condensed milk

½ cube butter

½ teaspoon vanilla

1 cup chopped nuts (walnuts or pecans)

Combine chips, sweetened milk, butter, vanilla in a bowl and microwave on medium heat for 30 seconds. Stir and repeat microwaving in intervals until melted and smooth.

Stir in nuts and spread in a prepared pan. Refrigerate for 1 hour and set on a counter for 1 hour.

Cut into 1-inch squares and store with waxed paper between layers in an air-tight container.

LIZ'S FUDGE

This is my cousin, Elizabeth Talarico's, fudge recipe. It is as easy as the Easy Fudge recipe. The consistency of this fudge is very dense. This is for true chocolate lovers. A square of this is a chunk of chocolate delight.

1 cup Eagle Brand condensed milk

2 cups chocolate chips

1 cup semi-sweet chips

Pinch of salt

1 ½ teaspoons vanilla

1 cup chopped nuts (optional)

Line 8x8 pan with waxed paper on all 4 sides, leaving an overhang for handles.

In a heavy saucepan on low heat add condensed milk, chocolate chips, and salt. Constantly stir until chocolate is melted and mixed. Remove from heat and add vanilla and stir in nuts.

Pour into prepared pan and refrigerate for one hour and then set on counter for one hour. Remove from pan, cut into 1-inch squares and store in airtight container with waxed paper between layers.

Eleanor Gaccetta

MRS. SEE'S FUDGE

The story behind this recipe is interesting. My mother's sister, our Aunt Mella, lived in California during the 1950's and 1960's with her husband, our Uncle Johnny. She had a neighbor who worked for Mrs. See's candy and who had a major altercation with her employer. In her anger and resentment, she shared the company's signature fudge recipe broadly with her family, friends, and neighbors. My aunt immediately shared it with my mother, and I would imagine that it has been shared many times over. My mother made this huge batch of fudge for many holidays and it was always a favorite. You can still buy Mrs. See's Fudge but now you can also make your own! Today such a story would have had a legal ending, but not then.

Spray 9x13x2 glass dish with non-stick spray and set aside.

4 ½ cups sugar

1 can evaporated milk

2 cubes butter softened

3 8 oz. packages chocolate chips

1 8 oz. jar marshmallow cream

2 teaspoons vanilla

2 cups chopped nuts–walnuts or pecans

In a large heavy pan boil sugar and evaporated milk for 10 minutes. Remove from heat and using a wood spoon add butter, chocolate, marshmallow cream, vanilla, and nuts. Stir until well mixed.

Pour into prepared dish. Refrigerate for 1 hour. Let it stand on counter for 1 hour and cut into1-inch squares.

Store in air-tight container with waxed paper between the layers.

PEANUT BUTTER SNOWBALLS

This is a great variation of peanut butter balls for a holiday. This recipe calls for white chocolate. But dark chocolate can be easily substituted.

This recipe can be easily doubled.

1 cup powdered sugar

½ cup peanut butter

3 Tablespoons butter softened

1 lb. white chocolate chips

Chopped nuts (optional)

Combine butter, sugar, and butter in a bowl. Chill in the freezer for 30 minutes. Roll into 1-inch balls and place on a baking sheet lined with waxed paper. Freeze 30 minutes.

In a double boiler or microwave melt the white chocolate and dip balls.

Place on waxed paper lined cookie trays and harden. Store in air-tight container with waxed paper between the layers.

POTATO CHIP CLUSTERS

This is a crazy, easy recipe that can be made anytime. This is a sure way to indulge the sweet and salty cravings of your family and friends.

9 oz. white chocolate chopped

2 cups crushed ridged potato chips (can use shoestring potatoes or Fritos)

½ cup pecans chopped

In a large bowl melt chocolate in a microwave. Stir in chips and nuts. Drop by Tablespoon on a baking sheet lined with waxed paper. Refrigerate until set.

THREE CHOCOLATE FUDGE

This recipe makes 5 ½ pounds of fudge.

1 Tablespoon butter

3 1/3 cups sugar

1 cup brown sugar packed

1 12 oz. can evaporated milk

1 cup (2 cubes) butter cubed

32 large marshmallows halved

1 teaspoon vanilla

2 cups semi-sweet chocolate chips

14 oz. milk chocolate chopped

2 oz. semi-sweet chocolate chopped

2 cups pecans chopped

Line a 15x10x2 pan with foil; grease with 1 Tablespoon butter and set aside.

In a large, heavy saucepan, combine sugar, milk, and cubed butter. Bring to a rolling boil over medium heat stirring constantly cook and stir for 5 minutes.

Remove from the heat, stir in marshmallows and vanilla until blended. Gradually stir chocolate until melted. Fold in pecans.

Spread into prepared pan and refrigerate for 1 hour until firm.

Remove from pan using foil handles and cut into 1-inch squares. Store between layers of waxed paper in air-tight container.

Tip:

For smooth, shiny fudge work quickly when spreading into the pan. Touch as little as possible.

For fudge pieces without ragged edges, clean your knife between cuts.

TIGER BUTTER

This is a peanut butter fudge that makes a nice addition to any holiday line-up. It is easy to make which is great for the novice candy-maker!

2–1 lb. bags of white chocolate chips

½ cup peanut butter

½ cup semi-sweet chocolate chips

Prepare 8-inch pan with foil on all sides with a 2 inch overhang for handles.

In a double-boiler melt white chocolate and peanut butter. Pour melted mixture into prepared pan.

Return double boiler to heat and melt semi-sweet chips. Spoon in mounds over mixture and run spoon through to make a marbled pattern.

Freeze one hour. Cut into squares and store in air-tight container with waxed paper between layers.

CPSIA information can be obtained
at www.ICGtesting.com
Printed in the USA
BVHW060625230321
603242BV00010B/824

9 781953 616975